Guide to
Strategic Planning

McGraw-Hill Finance Guide Series

Charles D'Ambrosio, *Consulting Editor*

Bowlin, Martin, and Scott: Guide to Financial Analysis
Gup: Guide to Strategic Planning
Smith: Guide to Working Capital Management
Weston and Sorge: Guide to International Finance

Guide to Strategic Planning

Benton E. Gup

Professor of Finance
College of Business Administration
University of Tulsa

McGraw-Hill Book Company

New York   St. Louis   San Francisco   Auckland   Bogotá   Hamburg
Johannesburg   London   Madrid   Mexico   Montreal   New Delhi
Panama   Paris   São Paulo   Singapore   Sydney   Tokyo   Toronto

This book was set in Press Roman by Automated Composition Service, Inc.
The editors were Bonnie E. Lieberman and Frances A. Neal;
the production supervisor was Charles Hess.
The drawings were done by VIP Graphics.
Fairfield Graphics was printer and binder.

GUIDE TO STRATEGIC PLANNING

1 2 3 4 5 6 7 8 9 0   FGRFGR   8 9 8 7 6 5 4 3 2 1 0

Library of Congress Cataloging in Publication Data

Gup, Benton E
    Guide to strategic planning.

    (McGraw-Hill finance guide series)
    Includes bibliographies and index.
    1. Business enterprises—Finance. 2. Corporations
—Finance. I. Title. II. Series.
HG4011.G84   658.1'5   79-21904
ISBN 0-07-025210-6
ISBN 0-07-025211-4 pbk.

To the Tulsa bankers who provided financial support for my research activities. Without their help this book would not have been possible.

Contents

2

EVALUATING A FIRM'S ENVIRONMENT

3
FINANCIAL DECISIONS

4

STRATEGIES FOR GROWTH

Preface

In the preface, authors typically explain what their book is about, how it differs from the competition, and who should read it. I am going to break with tradition and include all that material in the Introduction. This preface is short and to the point. Strategic planning is a hot topic because the world we live in is changing rapidly and organizations have to know how to cope with changes. In recent years, there has been dramatic progress in strategic planning, in terms of both the development of techniques and sophisticated corporate applications. This book emphasizes the financial aspects of the new and exciting techniques of strategic planning. It will enable you to play a major role in planning your company's needs for funds and in committing those funds to effective use because you will understand the problems and opportunities of corporate strategies. The book is practical and comprehensive. It is designed to give you the necessary tools to evaluate major corporate strategies with confidence.

I want to take this opportunity to express my thanks to Keith V. Smith of the University of California, Los Angeles and Charles A. D'Ambrosio of the University of Washington, who provided constructive comments, suggestions, and ideas that added significantly to the quality of this book. In addition, I want to thank my wife Joanne for her continued support.

Benton E. Gup

Guide to
Strategic Planning

Introduction

Benefits of Strategic Planning
  Survival
  Profits
  Improved Decision Making
  Avoid Mistakes

Strategic-Planning Techniques

About the Book

Introduction

New Perspectives

I was lecturing on valuation techniques at a seminar on strategic planning when one of the participants began squirming in his chair and mumbling to himself. During the next coffee break, he said to me, "You presented some ideas that really upset me. I discovered that one of my companies was sold way too cheaply because it was not valued correctly. It's too bad that I didn't take this seminar last year; it would have saved me a lot of money." This incident typifies the experience of those who are learning about the techniques of strategic planning. They discover new perspectives and new approaches for evaluating strategies.

BENEFITS OF STRATEGIC PLANNING

Before explaining the unique features of this book, let's examine some of the major benefits of strategic planning. According to *Business Week*, "Accurate planning has never been more necessary than in today's fast-changing economic environment."[1] Strategic planning permits organizations to react quickly in a

[1] "Corporate Planning: Piercing Future Fog in the Executive Suite," *Business Week*, Apr. 28, 1975.

3

dynamic environment, to explore more alternatives, and to develop new techniques. Strategic planning is a key to survival, profits, improved decision making, and avoiding mistakes.

Survival

We are living in a world of increasing uncertainty as evidenced by oil embargos, new government regulations, new technology, and increased foreign competition. These and other factors must be evaluated today in order to develop plans for reacting to them appropriately when they occur. For example, the major oil companies recognized that there is only a limited supply of oil left on this planet and that most of that supply is controlled by foreigners. In order to assure the survival of their organizations, they are diversifying into other energy sources such as coal, and into unrelated lines of business.

Profits

Strategic planning per se does not add to profits. However, a recent survey[2] concerning corporate models revealed the following benefits:

- Ability to explore more alternatives
- Better-quality decision making
- More effective planning
- Better understanding of the business
- Faster decision making
- More timely information
- More accurate forecasts
- Cost savings

It is the combination of all these factors that contributes to higher profits.

Improved Decision Making

Strategic planning encourages the evaluation of many different factors at the same time. For example, Dow Chemical Company monitors the costs of 140 raw materials on a weekly basis, and uses the data in its corporate model. Hewlett-Packard Company ran 100 different scenarios as part of its planning process to decide if the company should sell $100 million of long-term debt. Xerox makes alternative scenarios for 25 years into the future![3] This brief list is intended to demonstrate that strategic planning is used in a variety of ways to make decisions. The decisions that are made today will affect the future. Although the future is a moving target, strategic planning will improve your aim.

---

[2] Thomas H. Naylor, "The Future of Corporate Planning Models," *Managerial Planning*, March/April 1976, pp. 1–9.

[3] *Business Week*, loc. cit.

Avoid Mistakes

The city of Miramar, Florida, purchased a new fire truck. However, the city council did not budget $173,309 to pay for it. To make matters worse, the 44-foot-long truck was 6 feet longer than the firehouse; and it was too big to make the turn into the narrow street on which the firehouse is located.[4] This mistake could have been avoided by planning.

STRATEGIC-PLANNING TECHNIQUES

The necessity for strategic planning and its benefits are abundantly clear. Therefore, let's focus on how *Guide to Strategic Planning* can help you evaluate strategies. *Guide to Strategic Planning* differs from other books about strategic planning in two important respects. First, it emphasizes *techniques* that are used to evaluate strategies. Second, it emphasizes *financial techniques*. Although many books have been written about strategic planning, they are generally concerned with organizing for planning, the role of the chief executive, interrelationships between planners and managers, and other topics. This book does not cover those topics. *Guide to Strategic Planning* explains how to go about strategic planning and some of the major techniques that are used to evaluate strategies. The techniques are explained in easy-to-understand language, and there are a lot of examples. This is important because many people who are involved in planning have backgrounds in engineering, accounting, production, finance, and other areas and have not been exposed to the concepts that are presented here.

The techniques that are presented come from a wide variety of sources. Some of the techniques are taught in finance courses in universities but are rarely applied to strategic planning. Since only a relatively small portion of the population has attended college and an even smaller portion has taken college-level finance courses in recent years, the financial orientation of the decision-making techniques should provide some unique insights. Interestingly, other books dealing with strategic planning pay only lip service to the financial aspects of strategic decisions. This is unfortunate, because some strategies must ultimately generate profits if a firm is to survive.

Other techniques that are presented here are those used by major corporations and by consulting firms. A word of caution is in order at this point. The first chapter of this book explains how to begin strategic planning. Once when lecturing on that subject, I was interrupted by one of the students who said, "You are all wrong, that is not the way we do it at our company." The student worked in the planning department of a medium-sized oil company that was just getting started in planning. I explained that planning is an evolutionary process and that it takes time to perfect planning skills. In fact, it may take

[4]"New Fire Truck False Alarm: City Fails to Budget $173,309," *Tulsa World*, Aug. 28, 1976.

5 years or more from the time an organization decides to plan until it has a smoothly functioning planning process. Thus the methods used when a firm is just beginning to plan will be significantly different from those used by a firm that is experienced in planning. The techniques that are explained in Chapter 1 and elsewhere in the book are those that are used by firms that have already developed their planning skills. Therefore, do not be surprised or upset if your organization operates differently. After all, one of the objectives of this book is to give new perspectives and new approaches for making intelligent strategic decisions.

ABOUT THE BOOK

Guide to Strategic Planning is divided into four parts. Part 1, Introduction to Strategic Planning, consists of two chapters. Chapter 1 defines strategic planning and explains how an organization should begin the strategic planning process. Chapter 2 is about the product life cycle. This basic concept is very important in the planning process, and it is used extensively throughout the book. Part 2 explains techniques that are used to evaluate the environment within which firms operate. The environment includes existing markets, financial condition of the firm, the economic outlook, and many other factors. These factors must be evaluated as threats to the firm or opportunities for the firm. In either case, the firm must decide what actions, if any, to take in response to the threats or opportunities. Part 3 explains financial techniques that may be used to evaluate strategies, and techniques for determining the value of firms. In addition, it explains the use and limitations of models.

Part 4 explains strategies for growth. The notion of growth is stressed throughout the book. There are several compelling reasons why strategies for growth are important. First, growth is necessary to provide people with what they want. Stockholders want higher earnings and dividends. Employees want higher salaries, and management wants to retain their jobs. It is difficult to conceive of management stating that "it is philosophically opposed to growth; therefore, there will be no changes in earnings, dividends, or wages." Such a management would be replaced quickly. Second, growth can be justified on the basis of competition and survival. A firm must have sufficient size and capital in order to compete effectively. Along this line, the firms with the greatest production experience, or the largest firms, tend to have the lowest production costs and are the most profitable. Accordingly, the chapters in Part 3 explain how to manage a firm's financial structure and dividend policy, experience curves, portfolio strategies, and portfolio theory. The last chapter consists of a case study of the Mead Corporation. This chapter integrates some of the concepts that were explained earlier and describes the evolution of the planning process that is occurring at Mead.

If I were to select a new title for this book, it would be *Techniques of Strategic Planning* or *New Perspectives in Strategic Planning*. Both these titles, as well as the existing one, *Guide to Strategic Planning*, convey the idea of the content of the book. The titles also suggest who the potential readers of this book may be. However, in this regard, the titles are somewhat misleading. Obviously, strategic planning is important to executives, managers, and owners of business concerns. It is also important for those who operate nonprofit organizations and various government bodies. This is so because many of the planning tools are universal; they can be applied to many different types of planning situations and are not limited to one industry or one firm. Finally, this book is important to students who are studying business policies and strategies, and financial policies and strategies.

Part One

Introduction to Strategic Planning

There is a right way and a wrong way to begin strategic planning. This part of the book explains the right way to begin strategic planning. It consists of two chapters. The first chapter describes the process of strategic planning in terms of three questions that must be answered if planning is to be successful. The second chapter concerns the product life cycle. It is a very important tool in strategic planning and is used extensively throughout the book.

Chapter 1

Begin Strategic Planning by Asking Three Questions

Many business concerns and nonprofit organizations want to use strategic planning but they do not know what it is, or how to begin the process. The terms "strategy" and "strategic planning" are defined in various ways. Alfred Chandler defined strategy as "the determination of basic long-term goals and objectives of an enterprise, and the adoption of courses of action and the allocation of resources necessary for carrying out these goals."[1] Peter Drucker defined strategic planning as "the continuous process of making present entrepreneurial (*risk-taking*) *decisions* systematically and with the greatest knowledge of their futurity; organizing the *efforts* needed to carry out these decisions; and measuring the results of these decisions against the expectations through organized, *systematic feedback*."[2] Both statements deal with the same topic, but from different perspectives. In order to avoid arguments over semantics, the terms strategy and strategic planning as used here refer to major action programs that are used by an organization to achieve its mission and goals.

[1] Alfred D. Chandler, Jr., *Strategy and Structure: Chapters in the History of the Industrial Enterprise.* Cambridge, Mass.: The M.I.T. Press, 1962, p. 13.
[2] Peter F. Drucker, *Management: Tasks, Responsibilities, Practices.* New York: Harper & Row, Publishers, Incorporated, 1974, p. 125.

Having defined strategic planning, it is equally important to point out what is *not* strategic planning. According to Peter Drucker, strategic planning is not:[3]

1 The application of quantitative techniques to business decisions. It is analytical thinking and a commitment of resources to action.

2 It is not forecasting. In fact, strategic planning is necessary *because* we are unable to forecast beyond a short time span with any degree of precision. Entrepreneurs upset forecasts by bringing about innovations that by definition alter the course of economic, social, and political events.

3 Strategic planning does not deal with decisions that are made in the future. It deals with decisions that are made today that will affect the future.

4 Strategic planning does not eliminate risk. It helps management weigh the risks that it must take.

One way to begin strategic planning is by asking the proper questions. This chapter deals with three questions that must be asked by top management. The first question focuses on the direction that the company is going. The second question concerns the environment that the company must operate in. The final question deals with the strategic choices that the company must make.

WHERE ARE YOU GOING?

There is a saying that "if you do not know where you are going, it does not make any difference what road you take to get there." This saying has important implications for management because unless they know where they want to go strategic planning is a waste of time! To determine where a company is going, management must develop (1) a corporate mission, (2) a scope of operations, and (3) specific goals or objectives.

The Corporate Mission

Defining the corporate mission is the most important decision in the planning process because the purpose of the corporate mission is to state the nature of the company's business. The mission can be defined narrowly or in broad general terms, as demonstrated by Table 1-1.

The breadth or narrowness of the corporate mission has an important effect upon operations. A good illustration of this is the Mobil Corporation. Mobil has been known as an oil company for most of its history. The mission of an oil company is to produce and sell oil and related products. However, dramatic changes in the oil economics of the world in recent years have caused management to reappraise their corporate mission. Today, Mobil is an *energy* com-

[3]Drucker, op. cit., pp. 123–125.

Table 1-1   Corporate Missions

Narrow lines of business	Broad lines of business
Oil	Energy
Banking	Financial services
Soap	Personal hygiene products
Newspaper	Communications
Guard service	Security
Movie theater	Entertainment

pany instead of an *oil* company. The word "energy" has a broader meaning than the word "oil," since "energy" includes oil, gas, coal, the sun, nuclear power, and other sources. In addition to becoming an energy company, Mobil implemented a diversification program that included the following acquisitions: one of the world's largest retail stores (Montgomery Ward), the nation's largest manufacturer of paperboard packaging (Container Corporation), real estate developments, and chemical companies.

Another example concerns banks that have formed holding companies in order to broaden their lines of business. Bank holding companies are permitted by the Board of Governors of the Federal Reserve System to engage in the activities listed in Table 1-2, as well as other activities. A bank holding company located in New York City can own a finance company or a mortgage banking company that has offices located through the United States. Thus the bank holding company can operate in a wider geographic area than a "traditional" bank. Note that all the activities of the holding companies are closely related to banking. In contrast, it is difficult to see the common thread between an oil company (Mobil), Montgomery Ward, and Container Corporation. Such combinations create more complex problems for planners and management than business concerns that have a common thread. The important point is that the definition of the corporate mission determines the broad limits of a company's growth.

Table 1-2   Selected Activities of Bank Holding Companies

Finance company
Mortgage banking companies
Factoring companies
Leasing companies
Underwriting credit life insurance
Data processing
Operating an industrial loan company
Investing in community development projects

Source: Regulation Y, *Federal Reserve Bulletin*.

Scope

The corporate mission tells *what* business a company is in and the scope tells *where* they are doing business and their product market. For example, the mission and scope of First National City Corporation is to "provide any worthwhile financial service *anyplace* in the world permitted by law."[4] Most business concerns have a less ambitious geographic scope. One reason for the limited geographic scope is that many companies are regulated by federal or state governments. Regulations dictate where the airlines can fly, where banks can establish branches, where trucks can haul commodities, and where many other businesses of a "quasi-utility" nature can operate. Other factors that limit the scope of a corporation's business activity are transportation costs, location of natural resources, availability of labor and customers, and competition. Although this list is not exhaustive, it is sufficient to demonstrate that many factors limit the geographic area that a business services.

The concept of "scope" also refers to particular product markets. Many industries contain such a wide range of products that some companies specialize in one or two products. The fast food industry, for example, consists largely of firms that specialize in hamburgers, pizza, fish, Mexican food, or other specialty foods. Thus the product-market scope for Pizza Hut is pizza.

Goals

Once the mission and scope are established, it is necessary to determine specific goals. Such goals should be defined clearly in order to avoid ambiguity. To say that the goal is "growth" or a "reasonable rate of return" raises questions about what is meant by growth and what is a reasonable rate of return. This problem can be avoided by stating explicit goals such as those shown in Table 1-3. For example, the rate of return on assets should be 13 percent. However, not all corporate goals can be measured in terms of dollars. The goals could be to obtain a particular market share or a certain number of stores. Equally important, social goals and those dealing with constituents (customers, employees, suppliers, etc.) may have to be stated in general terms. "To assure a challenging and satisfying work environment for our employees, compensating them accordingly for their services and recognizing them for outstanding dedication to the Association"[5] is an example of such a goal.

---

[4]Statement by Walter B. Wriston, October 1970, emphasis added by author, appears in Alexander A. Robichek, Alan B. Coleman, and George H. Hempel, *Management of Financial Institutions: Notes and Cases*, 2d ed. Hinsdale, Ill.: The Dryden Press, Inc., 1976, p. 616.
[5]*1976 Annual Report*, Sooner Federal Savings and Loan Association.

Table 1-3 Corporate Goals for the Next 5 Years

1	Earnings per share—growth trend	15%
2	Sales growth trend	15%
3	Return on sales	7%
4	Return on total assets	13%
5	Return on investments	21%

Corporate goals are not static like words carved in granite. They should be changed when conditions, management, or the stockholders demand change.

In summary, the corporate mission, scope, and goals make it clear where the company wants to go. The next task is to determine how to achieve the corporation's goals.

WHAT IS THE ENVIRONMENT?

Before determining the strategies to achieve particular goals, it is necessary to analyze the internal and external environment within which the company operates. The purpose of this analysis is to provide information about a company's strengths, weaknesses, potential threats, and opportunities.

Introspection

Introspection is one of the first steps in planning. The term introspection means self-examination. The function of introspection is to determine the current *internal* condition of the firm and its existing markets. Introspection consists of a management audit, an examination of the firm's financial condition, and an analysis of their existing markets and strategies. It provides answers to the following questions. Is management capable of coping with future challenges? Are personnel recruitment, compensation, and training programs good enough to attract and retain the people who are required to achieve the corporate goals? How strong is the firm's balance sheet and what is the quality of earnings? Can existing markets yield greater profits? As a result of introspection, one bank discovered that it was doing a poor job cross selling its products. Very few of the depositors were borrowers from the bank, and very few of the borrowers had deposits at that bank. This discovery led to a strategy to improve cross selling. Another firm discovered that reducing its debt-to-equity ratio from 40 to 30 percent debt would result in increasing the rating on its debt securities from A to Aa. Finally, a major bank found that the biggest obstacle to its growth was a shortage of competent people. Chapters 2 and 3 present techniques that can be used for introspection.

The External Environment

According to a leading authority on planning, "External forces not under corporate control are and will be dominant in determining corporate destiny."[6] In other words, management must understand changing social, economic, political, and technological developments that may affect them now and in the future. For example, the shock of the 1973 oil embargo forced many companies to evaluate their sources and uses of energy. Baker International Corporation, a major producer of tools for oil and gas exploration, analyzed the energy factors affecting them in two ways—one over a long time period and the other over a short time period.[7]

Baker International Corporation foresaw four important long-run trends. First, the world's standard of living is based on energy. Second, the world will be dependent on hydrocarbons for the remainder of the twentieth century. Third, there is an imbalance between those that use energy and those that supply it. Moreover, the capital generated by energy consumption is not being entirely reinvested in energy-resource development. Finally, only a finite amount of oil and natural gas is available for world usage.

In the short run, the production of oil and natural gas in the United States declined despite the rising demands for energy products. Furthermore, the economics and incentives of energy exploration remained in doubt while the government contemplated new regulatory policies. Finally, the cost of exploration continued to rise because of inflation and problems associated with drilling in frontier areas. Baker used this information to determine if the trends represented threats or opportunities for the future development of the company.

Threats and Opportunities

Changing economic and social conditions that threaten some firms may offer golden opportunities for other firms. For example, rising crime rates have contributed to the introduction of many new products and services such as burglar alarms, locks, TV monitors, and various types of security services. On the other side of the coin, many companies have to pay for the products and services mentioned to avoid being robbed. The net effect is reduced earnings for those companies. Accordingly, each trend or factor considered in the external environment has to be weighed as to whether it is a threat or an opportunity.

Evaluating Alternatives

Once threats or opportunities have been identified, the process begins of evaluating their costs and benefits to determine if they are feasible or if some alternative must be found. Each investment alternative must be evaluated on its own

---

[6]A statement by Michael J. Kami, President, Corporate Planning, Inc., presented at the Fifth International Planning Conference, Cleveland, Ohio, July 20, 1976.
[7]Baker International Corporation, *1976 Annual Report*.

merits. Such an evaluation may include a feasibility study, pro forma projections, and the discounting of future expenses and revenues to their present value. Then potential investments must be evaluated in a portfolio context in order to determine if any "synergy" exists, and how it affects the overall risk and returns of the firm. Financial tools that are used for evaluating alternatives and portfolio concepts are discussed in detail in later chapters.

The Gap

At this stage of the planning process, one should have a firm understanding of the gap that exists between the current position of the firm and the desired position. If it is insurmountable, the goals of the firm should be revised because they are unrealistic. However, if the gap can be closed by expansion or diversification of the firm, the next step is to develop appropriate strategies.

HOW DO YOU GET THERE?

The function of strategy is to provide a method for achieving particular goals. The following examples illustrate strategies that were used by Eastern Airlines to affect their *market share*.[8] These strategies were developed in response to actions taken by other airlines.

Develop Strategies

From Eastern's point of view, there were three strategic options that would affect market share. Option 1 was strategic superiority, which means giving the best possible service to customers. Such service includes on-time arrivals and departures, on-time in-flight service, and on-time baggage handling. Trans World Airlines (TWA) initiated such a program but has had to pay the price in terms of higher fuel bills and potential revenue losses due to missed connections. Therefore, in considering this option Eastern chose not to be the best in all its areas in the United States but rather to concentrate on Atlanta, where it chose strategic superiority by offering more flights from Atlanta than any other airline.

Option 2 is strategic equivalence, which means matching the competition. When National Airlines offered "no frills" flights, Eastern matched this competition by also offering "no frills" flights in order to protect its share of the market.

Option 3 is strategic inferiority, which means being inferior to the competition. Pan American World Airlines, which has reduced its employment and suspended services in a variety of markets, used this option. In addition, Pan American exchanged routes with TWA and American Airlines in an effort to reduce its scope of operations. Eastern chose not to use this strategy.

[8] A presentation by Alfred E. Brescia, Direction of Economic Research and Forecasting, Eastern Air Lines, Inc., before the Planning Executives Institute, Corporate Planning Conference, Atlanta, Ga., Mar. 17–18, 1977.

Each company must design a strategy that fits its needs. Thus Eastern Airlines chose to develop strategies to achieve a larger share of the market. Dart Industries, a manufacturer and marketer of consumer products, chemicals, and plastics, developed the following strategy to achieve certain *financial goals*.[9]

1 Correct or eliminate loss divisions.
2 Pursue new manufacturing efficiencies and cost controls.
3 Eliminate products that do not add to the profitability or to an improved return on investment.
4 Constantly improve the quality of our research programs.
5 Make new capital commitments which have the potential of a return that will contribute to the attainment of our goal—which is 15 percent return on stockholders equity.

These examples from Eastern Airlines and Dart Industries illustrated strategies to achieve market share and financial goals, respectively. In each case, the strategies met certain criteria for their respective companies. First, they were attainable; that is, the strategies were realistic and could be achieved in a reasonable period of time. Second, the strategies were compatible with other objectives of the firm. Finally, the strategies were definable, as they could be measured and traced. This is important because it allows management to observe the success or failure of their decisions.

Contingency Plans

An important part of developing strategies is to make contingency plans in order to shorten the reaction times needed in certain situations. Contingency planning keeps surprises to a minimum, since the threats and opportunities of the situations have already been examined. Consider the case of an East Coast manufacturing company that shipped its finished products throughout the nation on its own trucks. The transportation division of this company was moderately profitable until the sharp escalation of fuel prices following the oil embargo in 1973. The transportation division could not pass all the increased costs of fuel and operation on to its customers, and the division became unprofitable. The company sold the transportation division and used "piggyback" transportation, which carries trailers on railroad cars to distant destinations. In addition, the company analyzed the impact of another large increase in shipping costs. In other words, they developed a contingency plan. Their analysis of the situation revealed that if another large increase in shipping prices occurred, the company should develop regional distribution centers and ship their products in boxcar loads. As part of the contingency plans, a listing of warehouses, their storage capacities, and other relevant factors was developed for key cities.

[9]Dart Industries, Inc., *Annual Report*, 1975.

Operations Plans

Strategies must be followed by an operating plan that results in management action. Many companies use operating plans that span a 5-year period. The plans are detailed for the first year and become progressively less detailed and accurate for the following years. Figure 1-1 depicts the accuracy of a 5-year planning cycle in the form of a series of expanding circles. The greatest accuracy is in the smallest circle, which represents next year. The accuracy diminishes steadily as additional years are added. The idea behind a 5-year plan is to allow the company to track a particular goal, such as a 13 percent return on total

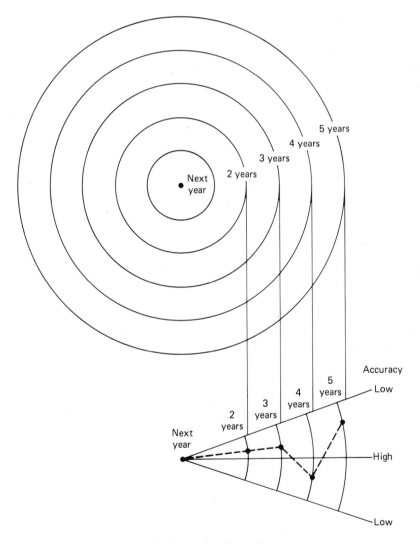

Figure 1-1   The accuracy of a 5-year planning cycle.

Table 1-4 Annual Planning Schedule

June	Corporate planners analyze environmental and industry factors	Marketing prepares sales forecast
July	Corporate planners analyze environmental and industry factors	Marketing prepares sales forecast
August	Corporate planners analyze environmental and industry factors	Marketing prepares sales forecast
September	Corporate planners analyze environmental and industry factors	Marketing prepares sales forecast
October	Planners and marketing adjust sales forecasts	
November December	Manufacturing prepares cost estimates and capital requirements	
January February	Corporate financial analysts examine pricing, distribution costs, gross margins, and financial analysis	
March April	Planners prepare 5-year plan	
May	5-year plan is presented to chief executive officer for critique	

assets, and move closer to that goal as the years unfold. There is nothing magic about the 5-year planning cycle. Some companies use 2-year planning cycles and others use 50-year time horizons, depending on the nature of their business. No matter what time horizon is selected, next year's plan is typically more accurate than plans for future periods.

Planning is a continuous process, and it takes time to develop operational plans. Table 1-4 presents the time schedule that is used for the preparation of the 5-year plan of a chemical producer. The company begins its planning process in June with an analysis of environmental and industry factors by the planning staff and sales projections by the marketing department. This phase of the planning process continues until the end of September. In October, adjustments are made in the sales forecasts based on discussions between the planning staff and the sales force. The revised sales forecasts are used for estimating the costs of manufacturing and capital requirements. These estimates are made by the manufacturing division during November and December. The corporate financial analysts then use all the above information to analyze pricing, distribution costs, gross margins, and general financial analysis of the forecasts. In March and April, the planning staff assembles all the relevant data and prepares a 5-year plan. The plan is presented to the chief executive officer in May, at which time the results of the past year's plan are reviewed and the new 5-year plan is critiqued.

The planning document or operational plan explains in considerable detail

Table 1-5 Elements of Strategic Planning

Questions		To obtain answers
1 Where are you going?	**a**	Determine the corporate mission
	b	Determine the scope of operations
	c	Establish specific goals
2 What is the environment?	**a**	Examine the internal condition of the firm
	b	Examine the external environment
	c	Analyze threats and opportunities
	d	Evaluate alternatives
	e	Measure the gap
3 How do you get there?	**a**	Develop strategies
	b	Develop contingency plans
	c	Develop operations plans, including procedures for reviews
	d	Implement plans with management action

who is responsible for particular functions and when they are to be accomplished. For example, the sales personnel are expected to contact two new customers each week. The manufacturing division is to acquire and install a new drill punch by April 15.

Finally, operating plans should provide for continuous or periodic review. If strategies are not working, they should be reviewed, analyzed, and changed if necessary.

CONCLUSION

This chapter outlined the major elements of strategic planning. The elements are grouped into three categories that are posed as questions. The questions and a summary of the elements of strategic planning are shown in Table 1-5. The first question deals with the mission, scope, and goals of the firm. This is the most important question. However, most of the time and effort in planning is spent on the next two questions. The second question explores the internal and external condition of the firm. The answers to this question provide information about the gap between the desired and current position of the firm, and about potential investment opportunities. The final question concerns several strategies that can be used to achieve particular goals.

This background provides a starting point for examining various strategic-planning techniques. The next part of the book explains techniques for analyzing the internal and external environment within which firms operate.

QUESTIONS[†]

1 Are budgeting and strategic planning the same thing?
2 How would you define the mission of McDonald's and Boeing?
3 What are the major factors influencing the external environment of virtually all firms today?
4 Are contingency plans important? Why?
5 Are 5-year plans expected to be accurate?
6 This is a bonus question. One of the objectives of this book is to change your perspectives. In order to test your current perspectives, connect all nine dots with four straight lines without lifting your pencil from the paper.

```
•     •     •


•     •     •


•     •     •
```

BIBLIOGRAPHY

Ackoff, Russell L. *A Concept of Corporate Planning*. New York: John Wiley & Sons, Inc., 1972.

Ansoff, H. I., R. P. Declerck, and R. L. Hayes. *From Strategic Planning to Strategic Management*. New York: John Wiley & Sons, Inc., 1976.

Carroll, Archie B. *Managing Corporate Social Responsibility*. Boston, Mass.: Little, Brown and Company, 1977.

Chandler, Alfred D., Jr. *Strategy and Structure: Chapters in the History of Industrial Enterprise*. Cambridge, Mass.: The M.I.T. Press, 1962.

Christopher, William F. *The Achieving Enterprise*. New York: American Management Association, 1974.

Drucker, Peter F. *Management: Tasks, Responsibilities, Practices*. New York: Harper & Row, Publishers, Incorporated, 1974.

Ewing, David. *The Human Side of Planning*. New York: The Macmillan Company, 1969.

———. *Long-Range Planning for Management*. New York: Harper & Row, Publishers, Incorporated, 1972.

Hirsch, Fred. *Social Limits to Growth*. Cambridge, Mass.: Harvard University Press, 1976.

Hussey, David. *Corporate Planning*. Oxford, England: Pergamon Press, 1974.

———. *Introducing Corporate Planning*. Oxford, England: Pergamon Press, 1971.

[†]Selected solutions at end of book.

McCarthy, Daniel J., Robert J. Minichiello, and Joseph R. Curran. *Business Policy and Strategy: Concepts and Readings*. Homewood, Ill.: Richard D. Irwin, Inc., 1975.

MacMillan, Ian C. *Strategy Formulation: Political Concepts*. St. Paul, Minn.: West Publishing Company, 1978.

Mockler, Robert J. *Business Planning and Policy Formation*. New York: Appleton-Century-Crofts, Inc., 1972.

O'Connor, Rochelle O. *Corporate Guides to Long-Range Planning*. New York: The Conference Board, 1976.

Regulating Business: The Search for an Optimum. San Francisco, Calif.: Institute for Contemporary Studies, 1978.

Schoennauer, Alfred W. *The Formulation and Implementation of Corporate Objectives and Strategies*. Oxford, Ohio: Planning Executives Institute, 1972.

Steiner, George A. *Top Management Planning*. New York: The Macmillan Company, 1969.

Taylor, Bernard, and John R. Sparkes. *Corporate Strategy and Planning*. New York: Halsted Press, 1977.

Toffler, Alvin. *Future Shock*. New York: Random House, Inc., 1970.

Chapter 2

The Product Life Cycle

The product life cycle is an analytical tool that can be used to determine the growth of sales and profit potential for products, companies, and industries. In addition, it provides information about financing requirements, dividend policy, and risk. Finally, the life cycle provides a frame of reference for analyzing strategies. Accordingly, it is used extensively throughout the book. The emphasis in this chapter and throughout the book is on growth. The reason is that growth and survival go hand in hand. Only the fittest firms survive, and they tend to be the largest ones. This chapter examines the concept of a life cycle, and suggests some of the ways that it can be used.

LIFE CYCLE

All products, companies, and industries evolve through stages of development called a *life cycle*. The life cycle is generally called the product life cycle. But the same concept applies to companies and industries. Thus the term life cycle is used in a general sense throughout the book. In some respects, the product life cycle is analogous to the development of a human being. In the early stages of human development, the rate of growth is rapid, and it then tapers off as adulthood approaches. After a relatively long period of maturity, some stagnation occurs. The product life cycle follows a similar pattern. By knowing what phase of the life cycle a firm or product is in, planners can develop appropriate strategies that will be presented shortly.

Pioneering Phase

The phases of development of the product life cycle are called *pioneering*, *expansion*, *stabilization*, and *decline*. They are shown in Figure 2-1. The first phase, *pioneering*, is characterized by the development and introduction of new products by a limited number of firms. Because production is small, and developmental costs have to be taken into account, the market price of new products is generally high. Some firms adopt a policy of "penetration pricing" in order to secure a large market share quickly. This means that they deliberately hold down

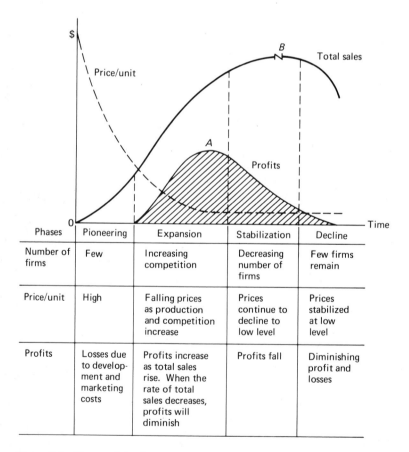

Phases	Pioneering	Expansion	Stabilization	Decline
Number of firms	Few	Increasing competition	Decreasing number of firms	Few firms remain
Price/unit	High	Falling prices as production and competition increase	Prices continue to decline to low level	Prices stabilized at low level
Profits	Losses due to development and marketing costs	Profits increase as total sales rise. When the rate of total sales decreases, profits will diminish	Profits fall	Diminishing profit and losses

Figure 2-1 Phases of development.

the selling price. Nevertheless, the typical new product has a high price; and in spite of the high price, there is a rapid expansion of sales fostered by a strong demand. Once the product is on the market, other firms recognize that there are ample opportunities for profit, and they enter the industry.

Expansion Phase

The second phase of the life cycle, *expansion*, is characterized by increased sales, production, competition, and falling prices. One result of the competition and lower prices is that some of the weaker firms fail or are absorbed by stronger firms. The process is like social Darwinism; only the fittest firms survive! Nevertheless, rising sales and profits continue to attract new firms into the industry. Profits are the difference between the revenues generated by sales and costs.

Although cost curves are not shown in the figure, costs deserve a few comments because managing costs are one key to survival. First, a firm maximizes its profits when, as the economists say, marginal revenue equals marginal cost. In plain English, this means that the greatest profits occur when the revenues from the last unit sold and the costs associated with that unit are equal. Beyond that point, the costs of each unit sold will exceed the revenue, and total profits will decline. Therefore, total sales revenues can increase but profits will decline. This is why Figure 2-1 shows that the point of maximum profit A precedes the point of maximum sales B.

Another aspect of cost concerns the relationship between cost and market share. In general, firms with the largest market share tend to have the lowest cost per unit. Therefore, when prices are falling sharply during the expansion phase of the life cycle, those firms with the highest costs per unit—which may be those with the smallest market share—have less chance of survival than those with lower costs. Accordingly, gaining market share and lower costs are important strategic considerations.

The pocket calculator is one example of a product and an industry that developed from the pioneering phase to the expansion phase in recent years. In the early 1970s, pocket calculators began to appear on the market, and they sold for $300 or more. They were an instant success, and the calculator boom began. In the first few years of the boom, an estimated 90 American and Japanese companies produced and marketed calculators under their own brand names.[1] By year-end 1974, it was estimated that one out of every ten Americans owned a pocket calculator. As production expanded, prices declined, and some units sold for $10 or less. The low prices had an adverse effect on profits, and many firms were forced out of business. After the shakeout that is still going on is complete, analysts estimate that fewer than ten firms will remain in the industry.

[1]Charles Hofer, "Toward a Contingency Theory of Business Strategy," *Academy of Management Journal*, vol. 18, no. 4, December 1975, pp. 784–810.

Stabilization Phase

Stabilization is the third phase of development. During this phase, sales increase slowly while prices and profits decline. In addition, the number of firms in the industry continues to diminish. By way of illustration, the automobile industry is in the stabilization phase of development. During the pioneering phase of this industry, there were hundreds of firms manufacturing automobiles. The prices of these early cars were considered "high" for their time. According to one source, during the expansion phase the number of firms may have reached 1500.[2] Today there are only four major domestic firms in the industry. As a general matter, the price of mass-produced automobiles is relatively low. The wide swings in industry profits reflect the cyclical nature of the demand for automobiles. In spite of the fact that the industry is mature, there was one new entrant in 1975. The Bricklin sports car was introduced to compete in the sports-car market. However, because of financial difficulties, Bricklin was forced to stop production.

Declining Phase

During the *declining* phase, sales decline and firms operate with losses. The rail-road industry is an example of a major industry on the decline. Nevertheless, their high fixed costs remained and increased over the years as a result of infla-tionary pressures. The net result was lower sales and losses for many railroads. Increasing competition for passenger traffic from automobiles and airlines re-duced railroad revenues.

DURATION OF CYCLES

The duration of a life cycle depends on many factors, including cost, technology, and the elasticity of demand for the product. For example, the coal industry was considered a declining industry until rising petroleum prices contributed to the rejuvenation of coal as a low-cost source of energy. The effect of tech-nology on life cycles is illustrated by the wristwatch industry. For many years, the demand for *mechanical* wristwatches was relatively stable. However, begin-ning in the early 1970s, watchmakers began to sell *digital* watches. As the technology improved and production increased, the prices of digital watches fell sharply. The reduced prices of digital watches affected the sales of mechan-ical watches because demand for wristwatches is highly "elastic." The *elasticity of demand* refers to the responsiveness of the quantity of a good that is de-manded to a price change. If the price of wristwatches declines 10 percent and the quantity demanded increases 20 percent, the demand is considered elastic. In contrast, if the price had declined and the quantity demanded had not

[2]Donald L. Kemmerer and C. Clyde Jones, *American Economic History*. New York: McGraw-Hill Book Company, 1959, p. 325.

changed, the demand would have been considered inelastic. The general concept of elasticity is important in evaluating the impact of price changes on the demand for products.

Substitutability of products is one of the factors that affects elasticity of demand and the duration of a cycle. For example, low-cost ball-point pens have largely replaced pens that use liquid ink. Similarly, hand calculators have replaced slide rules for engineers. Thus the life cycles for ink pens and slide rules were affected adversely by low-cost substitutes.

The duration and configuration of a life cycle may also be affected by *derived demand*. This means that the demand for one product creates demands for other products. For example, the demand for digital watches increased the demand for the semiconductors which are used to make watches. Similarly, if the demand for automobiles increases, steel, plastics, and textiles are a few of the industries that are affected.

Configuration of Cycles

The configuration of life cycles is not the same for all products or industries. Figure 2-2 shows two life cycles with different configurations. The top panel illustrates the life cycle of a product that is a "fad" such as hoola hoops or pet rocks. The sales of such products increase rapidly and then come to an abrupt halt when the fad ends. However, the sales of some fad products such as citizens

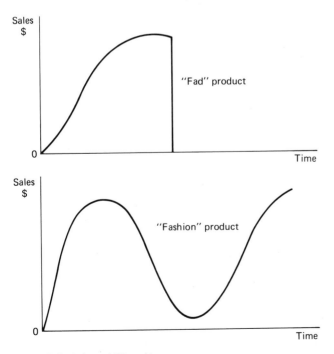

Figure 2-2 Selected life cycles.

band radios (CB) decline at a slower rate and then level off at a low level of sales.

The lower panel illustrates the life cycle of a "fashion" product such as long skirts. In the 1950s, long skirts were popular. They were out of fashion in the 1960s but they were back in vogue in the mid-1970s. Thus the sales of long skirts followed a cyclical pattern.

Location of Cycles

The location of a product, company, or industry at any point on the life cycle makes future rates of growth explicit. Figure 2-3 illustrates where the author believes selected companies and industries belong on a standard life cycle. Their placement was a matter of judgment because no precise method is available for making that determination. For example, National Semiconductor (NSM), a leading producer of electronic component parts, is in the early stages of the expansion phase. This implies that NSM sales will continue to expand rapidly. It also implies a high degree of risk, because many firms do not survive. McDonald's (MCD) is a firm that did survive and is an acknowledged leader in the fast food industry. As shown in the figure, MCD is in the advanced stages of the expansion phase. Procter & Gamble (PG) is an example of a firm that is in the early stages of stabilization, and Safeway (SA) is an example of a firm that is in the later stages of stabilization. For Safeway, this position suggests that sales will increase, but at a slow pace. Finally, Figure 2-3 also depicts the phase of development of three industries: the wristwatch, pocket calculators, and railroads. All three have been discussed.

Financial Considerations

Knowing the companies' position on the life cycle provides useful information about some of their cash requirements, dividend policies, and risk.

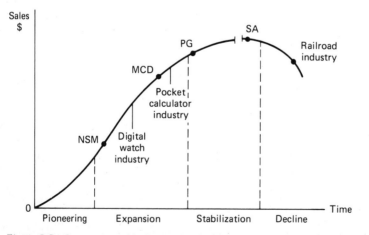

Figure 2-3 Company and industry development.

Table 2-1 Financial Considerations in the Phases of the Life Cycle

	Pioneering	Expansion	Stabilization	Decline
Cash requirements	Heavy cash use	Cash use	Cash generator	Generates surplus funds—until losses occur
Cash-dividend policy	No cash dividend	Small cash-dividend payout ratio—increasing	Increasing cash-dividend payout ratio	Large cash-dividend payout ratio—none if losses
Risk	High	High	Average	Low

Cash Requirements Companies that are in the pioneering phase of development tend to be heavy users of cash to fund research, development, and marketing efforts associated with new products (see Table 2-1). During the expansion phase of the cycle, there is still a strong need for cash because the company is expanding plant and equipment, and attempting to increase its market share. When the company enters the stabilization phase, the demand for cash, relative to the size of the firm, tapers off, and eventually the company generates surplus funds. During this phase of the cycle, some companies become "cash cows," which means that they have substantially more funds than they need.

Dividend Policy Dividend policies reflect cash requirements. During the pioneering phase of the cycle, companies generally lose money and there are no earnings to pay out as dividends. In the next phase of the cycle, earnings increase, but the demand for cash is still large; therefore, the cash-dividend payout ratio tends to be small. The dividend payout ratio is the cash dividend expressed as a percentage of earnings per share. Dividend payout ratios generally increase as companies mature. By way of illustration, consider the dividend payout ratios for National Semiconductor (NSM), McDonald's (MCD), Procter & Gamble (PG), and Safeway (SA) (see Table 2-2).

Table 2-2 Dividend Payout Ratios

Year	NSM (pioneering phase)	MCD (expansion phase)	PG (stabilization phase)	SA (stabilization phase)
1976	Nil	0.04	0.42	0.50
1977	Nil	0.06	0.43	0.56
1978	Nil	0.07	0.44	0.51

National Semiconductor is in the beginning of the expansion phase of the cycle. Therefore, it is a heavy cash user and pays no cash dividend. McDonald's is in the expansion phase of the cycle and paid its first cash dividend in 1976. Subsequently, the cash dividend increased. Nevertheless, the dividend payout ratio for McDonald's is still relatively low. In contrast, the dividend payout ratios for Procter & Gamble and Safeway, which are in the stabilization phase of the cycle, are substantially higher because their cash needs are relatively less than those of firms in the earlier stages of development.

Risk Stock-market investors' attitudes about the riskiness of a company can be associated with the life cycle. A statistic called beta is used as a measure of risk.[3] Beta measures the sensitivity of a stock's price to the overall fluctuations in the stock market. For example, a beta of 1.60 suggests that a stock tends to fluctuate 60 percent more (in either direction) than the stock market as measured by the New York Stock Exchange Composite Average or some other stock-market indicator. A beta of 1.10 suggests that a stock tends to fluctuate 10 percent more than the stock market. A beta of 1.00 implies that the stock behaves the same as the stock market as a whole. With respect to the life cycle, the risk is greatest during the early phases of development and diminishes as a company matures. As shown in Table 2-3, this is the pattern of betas that is shown for NSM, MCD, PG, and SA.

[3]In statistical terms, beta may be defined as the slope b of a linear relationship between the expected "excess" returns over a risk-free rate of individual stocks and the expected excess returns of a portfolio of stocks, or as follows:

$$Er_{it} - R_{ft} = b_i(Er_{mt} - R_{ft})$$

where Er_{it} = expected return on security i in period t
$\quad R_{ft}$ = riskless rate in period t
$\quad Er_{mt}$ = expected return on the market portfolio in period t
$\quad\quad b$ = beta, or the systematic risk measure of a stock relative to the market portfolio

Beta is used again in the capital-asset pricing model in Chapter 8 and portfolio theory in Chapter 12.

Table 2-3 Betas and the Phase of Development

Common stock	Beta	Phase of development
National Semiconductor	1.70	Pioneering
McDonald's	1.50	Expansion
Procter & Gamble	1.00	Stabilization
Safeway	0.93	Stabilization

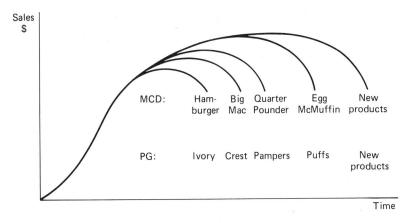

Figure 2-4 Extending growth with new products.

Altering Growth

Some companies can alter their rates of growth and the shape of their life cycles. For example, McDonald's and Procter & Gamble extended their life cycles by adding new products. As is shown in Figure 2-4, McDonald's (MCD) first started out with a basic hamburger. Subsequently, the product line was expanded to include Quarter Pounders, Big Mac, Egg McMuffin, and other products. Similarly, Procter & Gamble (PG) developed Ivory soap, Crest, Pampers, Puffs, and so on. Procter & Gamble adds new products and drops those that are no longer profitable. This method of growth demonstrates that some companies have considerable control over their destinies, and that movement from one phase of the life cycle to the next is not preordained.

Strategic Considerations

The examples of McDonald's and Procter & Gamble illustrate one type of strategy that is used in connection with the product life cycle. However, there are various strategies that can be used at each stage of the cycle to improve the chances of success. As shown in Table 2-4, during the pioneering phase, firms should try to minimize the learning process associated with introducing the new product, eliminate technical and marketing "problems," and gain widespread awareness of the benefits of the product.

During the expansion phase, the strategies are to obtain the maximum market share as soon as possible and to develop strong ties with dealers and cus-

Table 2-4 Selected Strategies

Phase of life cycle	Strategies
Pioneering	1 Minimize learning process
	2 Eliminate "problems"
	3 Gain market "awareness"
Expansion	1 Gain maximum market share
	2 Develop strong customer and dealer loyalty
	3 Enter new markets
	4 Product differentiation
Stabilization	1 Maintain and expand market share
	2 Enter new markets
	3 Product differentiation
	4 Diversification
Decline	1 Reduce costs
	2 Phase out

tomer loyalty for the product. In addition, firms may enter new markets and begin the process of product differentiation. Product differentiation means that there is a real difference between products or that customers imagine that there is a difference between them. Imagined differences are achieved by advertising or packaging.

During the stabilization phase, the primary objective is to maintain or expand the market share by entering new markets, improving the product, and differentiating it from competitors. Multiproduct firms who are at this stage of development may introduce new products. This is what McDonald's and Procter & Gamble did when they introduced Egg McMuffin and Puffs into the competitive scene. This is the phase of the cycle when promotional efforts must be directed toward maintaining strong dealer/franchise ties in order to maintain or expand market shares. During this phase of development, major changes in market share usually do not occur.

Diversification is another strategy that can be employed during the stabilization phase. For example, some tobacco companies have changed corporate missions and diversified into customer products such as fruit-flavored drinks, snacks, and other products. American Brands, Inc., obtained 67 percent of its operating revenue in 1977 from tobacco products and the remainder from food products (e.g., Sunshine crackers, Mott's applesauce), distilled beverages (e.g., Jim Beam bourbon, Mr. and Mrs. "T," Bloody Mary mix), Master Locks, and other consumer goods.

During the declining phase of the cycle, the strategy is to squeeze every last cent of profit out of the product. To some extent, this can be accomplished by reducing costs. At some time, the firm must phase out unprofitable products and markets. For example, the development of silicon chips and transistors has made electronic products using vacuum tubes obsolete. Therefore, manufacturers of vacuum tubes are reducing their inventories and will ultimately stop producing them.

CONCLUSION

The concept of a life cycle applies to products, industries, and organizations. The basic concept is that every product or industry evolves through certain phases of development, each phase having its own characteristics. The four phases that were examined are called pioneering, expansion, stabilization, and decline. Some of the characteristics that were examined for each phase are:

- Profits
- Competition
- Financing requirements
- Dividend policy
- Risk
- Strategies for growth

The life-cycle concept is a useful tool that when used properly provides valuable insights into the current development of products and organizations, and information about the future. For example, firms that are in the expansion phase of the life cycle should develop strategies to maximize their market share. Such strategies affect liquidity dividend policies and financial leverage. Some of the financial effects that were introduced in this chapter are explored in greater detail in later chapters.

QUESTIONS[†]

1 Does the concept of a life cycle apply to nonprofit organizations as well as business concerns?
2 List three companies that you consider to be in the pioneering phase of the life cycle.
3 What are the financial requirements of business concerns that are in the pioneering phase of the life cycle?
4 How can a business concern extend the duration of its life cycle?
5 What is the appropriate strategy for a business concern that is in the declining phase of the life cycle?

[†]Selected solutions at end of book.

BIBLIOGRAPHY

Argenti, John. *Corporate Collapse*. New York: Halsted Press, 1976.

Wasson, Chester R. *Dynamic Competitive Strategy and Product Life Cycles*. St. Charles, Ill.: Challenge Books, 1974.

Wells, Louis, ed. *The Product Life Cycle and International Trade*. Boston, Mass.: Harvard Business School, Division of Research, 1972.

Part Two

Evaluating a Firm's Environment

A firm's environment includes internal factors and external factors. Internal factors are those that can be influenced by the firm, such as the quality of management, plant, and equipment, and the allocation of financial resources. External factors are those that are beyond the control of the firm, such as economic conditions, wars, and weather. This part of the book explains how to evaluate both the internal and external factors. It consists of three chapters. Chapter 3 deals with introspection, which is the first step in the planning process. Chapter 4 explains how to evaluate the external factors as threats or opportunities. Chapter 5 is concerned with evaluating the financial condition of a firm.

Chapter 3

Chapter 3

Introspection: The First Step in Planning[1]

Introspection, the first step in the planning process, means self-examination. Introspection includes an evaluation of the financial condition of a firm, a management audit, and an analysis of existing resources and markets. The idea is to determine the strengths and weaknesses of an organization. Clearly, the strength of an existing organization is an important consideration in the planning process. Unfortunately, some planners overlook this crucial step in the planning process because they would rather focus on the future than on where they are at the present time. Without the benefit of introspection, the credibility of a plan is weakened and some potential opportunities for profit may be overlooked. By way of illustration, consider the case of the Golden State Bank, which used introspection to analyze the character of their existing accounts in order to learn more about the market in which they operate.[2] Although this case study focuses on an analysis of accounts and markets, it is sufficient to demonstrate some benefits of introspection.

[1] The chapter is based on an article by the author entitled "A Self Examination Plan for Smaller Banks," *The Magazine of Bank Administration*, May 1977, pp. 44–46.

[2] Although the names of banks used in this case study are fictitious, the data presented are based on actual bank studies.

GOLDEN STATE BANK: A CASE STUDY

Golden State Bank is located in the suburbs of a major metropolitan area. The bank was organized 5 years ago to serve the residential area that was developing at that time. Today, Golden State Bank has total deposits of $24 million. The president of the bank is satisfied with the past growth but is concerned about the future. The bank is currently in the expansion phase of its life cycle. Unless management acts quickly to meet competitive pressures, the bank's market share will erode, and its rate of growth will decline. Accordingly, as part of the planning process, the president wanted to know more about the quality of the existing accounts and the market that he deals in.

Sample Data

To obtain information about existing accounts, a sample of 150 customers, who had personal checking accounts, savings accounts, and loans, was selected at random in accordance with generally accepted statistical practices. The sample size was sufficiently large to provide a 95 percent accuracy. In other words, the chances are 95 out of 100 that the results of the study reflect accurately the characteristics of all the personal checking accounts of the bank. The data in the sample customers' accounts were examined for Wednesday, May 19, 1976, and for the entire month of May. That date was selected because it was not a payday, weekend, holiday, or any other unique day. It was just a "typical" day. Therefore, the results of the study should give a reasonable approximation of customer activity.

Number of Accounts

The 150 customers used in the sample had a total of 180 accounts with the bank because some customers had multiple accounts. The accounts were distributed as shown in Table 3-1.

The fact that only a relatively few customers had multiple accounts indicates that the bank could do a more effective job *cross selling* its services. The term cross selling means that customers with checking accounts should be sold other services including savings accounts, loans, safety deposit boxes, and so on. When the geographic location of the various accounts was plotted on the map that will be discussed shortly, it was revealed that the customers with loan accounts were distributed over a wider geographic area than those with checking accounts and savings accounts. Only two of the customers with loan accounts moved out of the area after they had obtained loans. In addition, the bank does not buy automobile loan contracts, commonly called "finance" paper, from automobile dealers. The fact that the loan customers are distributed over a wider geographic area than checking-account customers suggests that individuals will travel a considerable distance to shop for loans, but they want to stay relatively close to home or work for their checking-account needs.

Table 3-1   Number of Accounts

Type of account	Number of accounts
Checking	95
Savings	40
Loan	36
Closed	4
Dormant for 60 days	3
Certificates of deposit	2
Total	180

Multiple accounts	Percent distribution
Checking and savings	48
Checking and loan	42
Checking, savings, and loan	10
Total	100

CHARACTERISTICS OF ACCOUNTS

Checking Accounts

The data presented in Table 3-2 show the distribution of the current balances in checking accounts. In spite of the fact that the (arithmetic) average balance was $358, almost half of the accounts had balances of less than $100. The arithmetic average was biased upward by a $6678 balance in one of the accounts. The median—which means that half the values are above it and the other half are below it—provides the most realistic measure of central tendency in this case. The median value was $107.

Although it is not shown in Table 3-2, about one-fourth of the total number of accounts had balances of less than $20. The data revealed the fact that the

Table 3-2   Current Balance in Personal Checking Accounts

Balance	Percent
$ 0–$99	49.0
100–199	12.6
200–299	11.3
300–399	5.3
400–499	2.0
500–599	6.9
600 or more	13.3
Total	100.0

Range $0–$6,678
Average $358
Median $107

checking-account operations were run at a loss because the costs of operation exceeded the size of the average balance in the accounts.

According to the *Functional Cost Analysis* data provided by the Federal Reserve System, the average minimum balance in personal checking accounts with no service charge was $129. Functional cost data were developed to aid banks in maintaining uniform income and cost-accounting systems as a tool for bank management. The functional cost data revealed the break-even for all types of checking accounts including public funds was $1203.[3] Moreover, deposits of $200 or less accounted for 41 percent of the *total number* of accounts and about 2 percent of the *dollar volume* of checking accounts. However, deposits of $200 or less accounted for 61.6 percent of the dollar volume of checking accounts at Golden State Bank. These data indicate that significant effort should be made to increase the level of checking-account balances. Equally important, the bank established service charges on its checking accounts.

Savings Accounts

The data for the savings accounts revealed that 26 percent of the customers sampled had savings accounts at Golden State Bank. The size of the savings accounts ranged from $2 to $7345. The average balance in such accounts was $841 and the median was $285. Only 3 percent of the total accounts surveyed had balances in excess of $800. During the month, the dollar amount of withdrawals exceeded deposits by a wide margin. The opening of a branch office of a savings and loan association in close proximity to the bank may explain some of the withdrawals. In summary, the distribution of savings accounts was similar to the distribution of checking accounts because both types of accounts were dominated by small balances.

Loans

Sixteen percent of the customers sampled had installment loans outstanding. This proportion is comparable to other local banks. The average amount of loans outstanding was $4350. This number is substantially larger than the average loan size of $1731 that appears in the functional cost data. Most of the loans were made to purchase an automobile, and a small number of loans were made to purchase pleasure boats. The annual percentage rate charged on loans ranged from 8.56 to 16.83 percent, and the average was 11.42 percent. The relatively high average loan size and interest rate suggest that the bank should continue its efforts in marketing consumer loans.

Eight percent of the customers sampled had real estate loans. This percentage is relatively high but reflects the fact that the bank is located in an area where housing starts have increased sharply in recent years.

---

[3] *Functional Cost Analysis: 1975 Average Banks*, Federal Reserve System, 1976. Data used are for banks with deposits up to $50 million.

GEOGRAPHIC LOCATION OF ACCOUNT HOLDERS

The previous section highlighted some of the characteristics of various types of accounts. Now we will direct our attention to the account holders themselves in order to learn more about the banks' relevant market. Figure 3-1 depicts the percent distribution of the addresses of the 150 customers used in the sample. The data reveal that the greatest concentration of account holders is in the 4-square-mile area surrounding the Golden State Bank. For purposes of this analysis, this 4-square-mile area (indicated by shading on the map) is called the *primary market area* because it contains most of the customers (59 percent).

The map also shows that the number of customers drops off sharply in the areas located near the two competing banks. It is interesting to note that Golde State Bank has a larger proportion of customers near the Central Bridge Bank than near the 3d St. State Bank. At this point, it is not clear whether the 3d St. State Bank is a tougher competitor than the Central Bridge Bank or if natural traffic flows account for the difference.

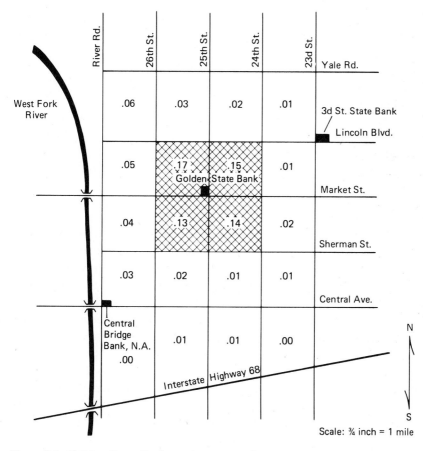

Figure 3-1 Golden State Bank market area and percent distribution of account holders (8% of customers located in areas not shown on map).

Finally, 8 percent of the customers live in areas that are not shown on the map. Most of these customers have only loan accounts with the bank.

THE PRIMARY MARKET AREA

The Golden State Bank is located in a growth area. The population in the primary market area increased from 5489 in 1960 to 12,370 in 1970. The City Planning Commission estimated that the population will double before the next census. The increased population was paralleled by increases in business activity and public services. For example, a new senior high school and a 50-bed hospital were recently constructed. Moreover, the primary market area contains 185 acres that are zoned for commercial use. This amount of acreage allows for 1.4 million square feet of floor space. A detailed listing of existing business concerns was also included in the study.

CONCLUSION

The introspection gave Golden State Bank useful insights about some of its own operations and the market in which it deals. The insights included information about the size of accounts, effectiveness (or lack thereof) of cross selling, the size of the primary market, and some growth projections for that market. Based on this information, the officers of the bank realized that they can increase the profitability of the bank by making better use of their existing customers. Recognizing that the bank is in the expansion phase of its life cycle, management strategies to increase the profitability of their existing accounts included developing strong customer loyalties and differentiating their services from those of competing banks.

The complete introspection study revealed some inadequacies in the design of the bank's drive-in window that made it difficult for customers to use that facility. It also revealed that the bank lacked management in depth. The chief executive officer, who had been with the bank since its inception 5 years before, wanted to be involved in virtually every decision that was made in the bank. This study convinced him that some of his responsibilities should be delegated to other officers and that an officer training program was needed to provide for management succession. Based upon all these findings, the management took corrective actions and was able to plan effectively for the bank's growth.

The introspection process does not assure that a firm will improve its profits or add to its market share. In most cases, introspection helps to avoid costly errors of attempting strategies that are not operationally or financially feasible. For example, the management of Highlands Storage and Transfer Company was considering adding 20,000 square feet of storage area to their warehouse. They believed that the additional capacity would allow them to compete for the accounts of Safeway and other food chain stores. Part of the introspection process consisted of evaluating existing customers' usage of their facilities. In doing so, they discovered that within the next year Eastman Kodak Company would consolidate its inventories in a company-owned warehouse and would no longer be using their facilities. The loss of this client would release a sufficient amount of space to make the building addition an unnecessary and unwise strategy at this time.

Finally, understanding the life cycle is important in the introspection process. Firms that are just entering the expansion phase, for example, will have different characteristics from those that are in the declining phase. By way of illustration, consider some of the financial characteristics that were explained in the previous chapter. Firms in the expansion phase may expect increasing profits, a high degree of financial leverage, and low liquidity; while those in the declining phase will have low financial leverage and high liquidity until the products become unprofitable.

QUESTIONS[†]

1 Explain the significance of the term "introspection."
2 Two firms are in the introspection phase of their planning cycles. One firm is in the early expansion phase and the other is in the late stabilization phase. How would the financial characteristics of each firm differ?
3 To what extent do the banks that you use cross sell their services?
4 The Golden State Bank case study focused on a market analysis. What else should be included in an introspection?
5 Develop some alternative strategies for Golden State Bank to increase their market share.

BIBLIOGRAPHY

Bradley, Stephen P., and Dwight B. Crane. *Management of Bank Portfolios*. New York: John Wiley & Sons, Inc., 1975.
Cross, Howard D., and George H. Hempel. *Management Policies for Commercial Banks*, 2d ed. Englewood Cliffs, N.J.: Prentice-Hall, Inc., 1973.
Erdman, Paul E. *The Crash of '79*. New York: Simon & Schuster, Inc., 1976.
Hayes, Douglas A. *Bank Lending Policies: Domestic and International*, 2d ed. Ann Arbor, Mich.: Division of Research, Graduate School of Business Administration, The University of Michigan, 1977.
Havrilesky, Thomas M., and John T. Boorman. *Current Perspectives in Banking: Operations, Management, and Regulation*. Arlington Heights, Ill.: AHM Publishing Corporation, 1976.
Jain, Subhash, and Surendra Singhvi, eds. *Essentials of Corporate Planning*. Oxford, Ohio: Planning Executives Institute, 1973.
Jessup, Paul E. *Innovations in Bank Management*. New York: Holt, Rinehart and Winston, Inc., 1969.
Nadler, Paul S. *Commercial Banking in the Economy*. New York: Random House, Inc., 1968.

[†]Selected solutions at end of book.

Chapter 4

Monitoring the External Environment
  Economic Factors
  Physical Factors
  Political Factors
  Social Factors
  Technological Factors

Impact Matrix
  Trends
  Events
  Constituents
  Missions and Strategies
  Measuring the Impact

Vulnerability Analysis
  Underpinnings
    Market Need / Resources / Customer Base / Stable Prices
    Technology / Special Abilities / Barriers to Entry
    Values–Integrity / Uniqueness
  Threats
  Probability and Impact

Organizational Response to Change

Conclusion

Questions

Bibliography

Appendix 4A Selected Sources of Statistical Data from Federal and State
        Governments

Appendix 4B Selected Sources for United States Market Statistics

Appendix 4C Sources for United States Financial and Operating Ratios

Chapter 4

Evaluating External Forces: Threats or Opportunities?

The growth of most firms is dominated by forces that are not under their control. For example, developments in electronic technology have spurred the growth of firms that make electronic calculators and digital watches and have contributed to the demise of some firms that made slide rules and mechanical wristwatches. Thus developments in electronic technology are an opportunity for some firms and a threat to others. Other external forces include increasing use of satellite communications, declining birth rates, increased participation by women in the labor force, increasing government regulations concerning pollution, and so on. To what extent are these and other external factors opportunities or threats? This chapter presents three methods for measuring the impact of threats or opportunities. The first method identifies particular threats and opportunities. The second method measures the impact of threats on the firm. The third analyzes how much effort is required to respond to threats or opportunities. At the end of the chapter are appendixes containing selected sources of data that may be helpful in evaluating external forces.

MONITORING THE EXTERNAL ENVIRONMENT

Everything that is outside the business firm is called the external environment. However, that concept is so broad that it is necessary to divide the external environment into categories that make the process of monitoring it relatively easy. The following five categories represent one way of categorizing factors in the external environment that can influence business concerns.

Economic Factors

This category includes the economic outlook, long-run economic projections such as continued inflation or the declining rate of return on capital investments. In addition, changes in competitive conditions may be included in this category.

Physical Factors

Mother Nature affects all of us, but she has a greater impact on some firms than on others. Shortages of certain natural resources, pollution, severe and unusual weather conditions, and a gradual cooling off of the Northern Hemisphere are crucial factors for many firms.

Political Factors

This category encompasses legislation, regulations, and political attitudes. For example, the political party in power might favor social reforms and welfare programs. Such a philosophy will result in increased federal support for health and welfare programs, and a reduction of spending on defense hardware.

Social Factors

Social modes change. And with the changed modes come changes in products and services. Social modes include attitudes about women working, divorce, sex, drinking, and many other factors that affect life style.

Technological Factors

There have been dramatic changes in technology in recent years, and more are forthcoming. The evolution of transportation from a 100-mile-per-hour airplane during World War I to a space shuttle traveling thousands of miles per hour is one example of technological change. The electronics revolution is another example of technological change. Today, a single silicon chip that is used in computers and calculators can perform 20,000 functions. By 1990, some experts estimate that a single chip will be able to perform 10 million or more functions.[1]

Merely observing changes in the external environment does not provide much useful information to business concerns. The observations have to be

[1] "Texas Instruments Shows U.S. Business How to Survive in the 1980s," *Business Week*, Sept. 18, 1978, p. 69.

evaluated in a meaningful way, and this can be accomplished by the use of an impact matrix.

IMPACT MATRIX[2]

The purpose of an impact matrix is to determine threats and opportunities facing the firm. The matrix reflects the impacts of trends, events, and the demands of its constituents on a firm's missions and strategies. Once this is accomplished, management can weigh the threats and opportunities to determine the appropriateness of its missions and strategies. As shown in Figure 4-1, the rows of the impact matrix consist of trends $(T_1, T_2, \ldots, T_n)$, events $(E_1, E_2, \ldots, E_n)$, and the demands of constituents $(C_1, C_2, \ldots, C_n)$. These three categories consist of relevant factors that were observed in the external environment. The word relevant is underscored because the factors should be limited to those that have some impact on the firm. For example, the rise in consumerism is a trend, but it may not be a relevant trend for the manufacturer of torpedoes and bombs.

Trends

The term *trends* refers to changes or movements that occur through time. There is a trend toward increasing government regulation of business. Along this line, by now most businessmen recognize that OSHA is not a small town in Wisconsin and ERISA is not a funny name in a comic strip. Both OSHA and ERISA are evidence of increasing government regulation. The acronyms OSHA and ERISA stand for Occupational Safety Health Act and Employee Retirement Income Security Act, respectively. Other trends may be industry-related. For example, there is a trend for large food chain stores to add prescription drug departments and sell some soft goods to make their stores more profitable.

Events

Events are important occurrences. They happen once, although they can happen over an extended period of time. Some examples of events are the oil embargo of 1973, the extremely harsh winter of early 1977, and the Vietnam conflict. Other events happen periodically, such as the election of a new president.

Constituents

Demands of constituents are the final category of external factors. Constituents include stockholders, customers, suppliers, employees, regulators, and others.

[2]This section of the chapter and the section on Organizational Response to Change draw on the work of F. Friedrich Neubauer (a faculty member of General Management and Corporate Planning at Le Centre d'Etudes Industrielles, Geneva) and of Norman B. Solomon (Associate Director, European Management Forum, Geneva), as well as a paper by Neubauer entitled "A Managerial Approach to Environmental Assessment," presented at the 5th International Conference on Planning, July 18–21, 1976, Cleveland, Ohio.

By way of illustration, consider the role of regulators in banking. If the regulatory authority sets a standard for the amount of capital required by banks, the banks will have to measure up to that standard.

Missions and Strategies

The columns of the impact matrix shown in Figure 4-1 consist of the firm's existing or proposed missions and strategies. The *mission* refers to the firm's lines of business. For example, Tenna Corporation manufactures and markets automotive accessories. The accessories include citizen-band antennas, automotive sound systems (tape players, radios, and speakers), mirrors, and fractional-horsepower motors. It may be useful to separate the several different product lines, because some trends may have a different impact on say citizens-band antennas than on automotive mirrors.

Strategies consist of major action programs that are used by the firm to achieve its mission and goals. Let's say that the mission of a bank holding company is to be a financial service organization. The strategies that can be employed to achieve that mission are (1) acquire more banks, (2) acquire a mortgage banking company, (3) acquire a consumer finance company, and (4) become an investment adviser.

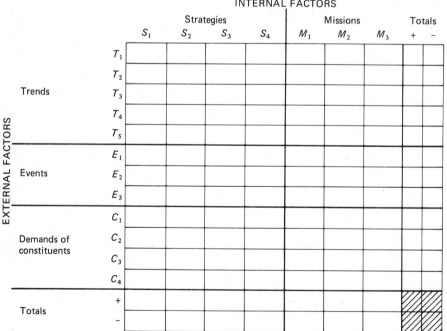

Figure 4-1 Impact matrix.

Measuring the Impact

The effect of each external factor on the firm's missions and strategies is measured on a scale that ranges from -5 to +5. The values that are assigned are based on *judgments* made by management. As shown below, the negative (-) impacts are threats to the organization. A -5 is a big threat and a -1 is a small threat. The term threat means that there is increased risk associated with a strategy or mission, or that the firm may be prevented from carrying out a strategy or mission. The positive (+) impacts represent opportunities. A +5 represents a large opportunity and a +1 represents a small one. An opportunity means that the external factor will have a favorable effect on the company. It can also mean that the firm might want to change some of its policies to exploit some new areas that are potentially profitable. A zero (0) impact means that the external force has no effect on the company. Finally, it is possible that an external force can have both a negative and a positive effect on the firm. For example, rising oil prices may have a negative effect on gasoline sales, but they increase the value of all the products sold, including petrochemicals, which were not sensitive to price changes. In this case, the impact might be recorded as say -4/+3.

Threats						Opportunities				
-5	-4	-3	-2	-1	0	+1	+2	+3	+4	+5
High impact				Low impact	No impact	Low impact				High impact

In order to demonstrate the measurement process, consider one strategy of an international metals company. The strategy is building a processing mill in South Africa. The company is considering building mills in other parts of the world too, but these strategies are not shown. Table 4-1 lists the impacts of selected trends, events, and constituents. The first trend is increasing demand for chromium and manganese. Both these metals are widely used in industrial processes. Equally important, the sources of these critical raw materials are limited to South Africa and several other foreign nations. Accordingly, the management gave this trend a score of +5 because building the mill will have a very beneficial effect on the company. The second trend is increasing prices for chromium and manganese. These price trends reflect the growth of industrial demand throughout the world for these metals, and the limited supply. Accordingly, the second trend was given a score of +5. The third trend is increasing restrictions on royalties. This trend will tend to lower the company's income over time; consequently it was given a score of -1.

The first event that is listed is the overthrow of the friendly host government. Although the management did not consider this to be a likely event

Table 4-1   Single Strategy and Selected Impacts
Strategy 6 (Build Processing Mill in South Africa)

		Impact
Trends		
T_1	Increasing world demand for chromium (Cr) and manganese (Mn)	+5
T_2	Increasing prices for Cr and Mn	+5
T_3	Increasing restrictions on royalties	−1
T_4	Other trend	−2
T_5	Other trend	−3
. .		. .
Events		
E_1	Overthrow of friendly host government	−3
E_2	Expropriation	−4
E_3	Devaluation of local currency	−2
E_4	Other event	−4
E_5	Other event	−2
. .		. .
Constitutents		
C_1	Increasing demands from local labor force	−1
C_2	Host government requiring local participation	−1
C_3	Other constitutent	−5
. .		. .
. .		. .
Total		−18

within the next 3 years, it would still have a negative impact (−3) on the company. The second event is expropriation, which was also considered unlikely; but it would have a more damaging impact on the company (−4). The next event shown is devaluation of the local currency, which would result in foreign-exchange losses and would have a negative (−2) impact on the firm.

Under the constituents category, the local labor force has been making increasing demands for higher wages and better working conditions. In addition, the host government is requiring increased participation by local investors. Both of these were given impacts of −1. When the impacts of all the trends, events, and constituents are summed, the total score after all the pluses (+) and minuses (−) have been taken into account is −18. This number indicates that the overall impact of strategy 6, building a processing mill in South Africa, is negative; and the firm should reconsider it. Of course, the total score cannot be considered in isolation. It must be compared with other total scores. More will be said about this shortly.

INTERNAL FACTORS

		Strategies					Missions			Totals	
		S_1	S_2	S_3	S_4	S_5	M_1	M_2	M_3	+	−
Trends	T_1	− 5	− 2	− 1	0	+ 2	0	− 1	− 4	+ 2	−13
	T_2	+ 4	0	0	0	+ 3	+ 1	+ 2	− 5	+ 9	− 5
	T_3	+ 5	+ 5	+ 4	+ 1	− 4	+ 5	+ 4	+ 2	+26	− 4
	T_4	− 4	− 4	− 3	− 5	− 3	− 3	− 1	+ 1	+ 1	−23
	T_5	+ 3	+ 1	+ 2	− 1	+ 1	0	+ 1	− 5	+ 8	− 6
Events	E_1	+ 4	+ 3	+ 5	+ 1	+ 5	-2/+3	+ 5	+ 3	+29	− 2
	E_2	+ 2	+ 2	+ 2	+ 5	+ 2	+ 3	+ 1	+ 2	+19	0
	E_3	− 5	− 2	+ 1	− 4	0	+ 4	0	+ 3	+ 8	−11
Demands of constituents	C_1	+ 5	+ 3	− 5	− 1	+ 2	+ 3	+ 1	+ 1	+15	− 6
	C_2	+ 1	+ 3	− 1	− 1	+ 1	+ 2	+ 4	− 4	+11	− 6
	C_3	0	− 1	+ 4	− 2	+ 3	+ 4	+ 2	− 5	+13	− 8
Totals	+	+24	+17	+18	+ 7	+19	+25	+20	+12		
	−	−14	− 9	−10	−14	− 7	− 5	− 2	−23		

EXTERNAL FACTORS

Figure 4-2 Sample impact matrix.

The process that was described for the single strategy is repeated for each of the firm's strategies and missions until the entire impact matrix is completed. A sample of a complete impact matrix of a forest-products company is presented in Figure 4-2. Note that every cell in the matrix is assigned a value indicating the impact of each external factor on each strategy and mission. For example, trend T_1 has an impact of −5 on strategy S_1 and an impact of 0 on mission M_1. Similarly, event E_1 has an impact of +4 on strategy S_1 and both a negative and positive impact (−2/+3) on mission M_1.

Once all the impacts have been recorded, the positive and negative values are totaled separately for each of the rows and columns. The totals reveal that three external factors (T_3, T_4, and E_1) are sufficiently large that they deserve further study by management. Both T_3 and E_1 are relatively large positive (+) numbers, indicating that they are opportunities. For example, T_3 is increasing worldwide demand for one of the firm's by-products. The total score of +26 indicates that the firm has an opportunity to profit from the by-product instead of paying to have it hauled away as trash. For many years, lumber mills disposed of their wood chips until they realized that wood chips could be used to make particle board and other products.

Trend T_4 has a large total negative impact (-23), indicating that it is a threat to the firm. Trend T_4 for the lumber mill is increasing government regulation of pollution. The extent to which threats may injure a firm can be estimated by vulnerability analysis, which is explained next.

VULNERABILITY ANALYSIS[3]

The impact matrix highlighted both opportunities and threats. Vulnerability analysis is a method that can be used to determine how susceptible an organization is to threats. The analysis is divided into three parts. The first part consists of determining the basic "underpinnings" of a business concern. The second part is concerned with the threats to those underpinnings, and the final part deals with the probabilities that those threats will occur by a particular date. When all this is accomplished, management will have a better insight into the problem areas that require immediate attention and those that require other types of action.

Underpinnings

Underpinnings means the basic foundations that a business depends on in order to operate effectively. The following is a list and brief explanation of nine underpinnings that are common to many types of business concerns and products.

Market Need Is there a need for the products or services being offered for sale? For example, there is a need for replacement tires because there are millions of automobiles in use that are wearing out their original-equipment tires.

Resources There are both external and internal resources. External resources include natural resources and basic supplies that are necessary for the production process. Internal resources include people, capital, and plant and equipment.

Customer Base Who are the customers that need the products or services? The customer base of a local public utility includes all the individuals and organizations within a given geographic area. The customer base for a publisher of college biology tests consists of all the students who are taking biology.

Stable Prices Many business concerns are dependent on stable prices and costs over a relatively long period of time. A construction firm that bids on a

---

[3] This section of the chapter is based on a presentation by Douglas A. Hurd and E. Riggs Monfort III, both of Stanford Research Institute, made at the 5th International Conference on Planning, July 18-21, 1976, Cleveland, Ohio.

large shopping-center complex that will take 2 years to build assumes that the costs of basic material will be relatively stable or increase at a known rate. Unless some flexibility with respect to prices is built into the bid, the contractor could lose money if prices rise unexpectedly.

Technology Changing technology had a dramatic effect on the wristwatch industry. In the 1950s, Switzerland was the leading producer of mechancial watches. In the 1960s, the tuning fork and quartz crystals became popular in watches and the United States and Japan began to produce watches in large volume. In the 1970s, semiconductor technology contributed to the development of digital watches, and the United States became the dominant nation producing watches. Thus a change in technology changed the structure and nature of an entire industry.

Special Abilities Some firms are known for their special abilities to produce a particular kind of product or service. For example, Lloyd's of London is known for handling high-risk insurance policies.

Barriers to Entry New firms can be barred from entering an industry and existing firms can be barred from new markets because of government regulations, high capital costs, lack of technical knowledge, and other factors. For example, one has to go through a lengthy and costly process in order to file an application for a new bank charter. Once the application is filed with say the state banking commission, protesting banks may convince the commission that the application is not in the best public interest, and it can be denied. The government granting new airline routes to existing airlines is an example of barriers to entering new markets.

Values—Integrity Some firms are known for their integrity. Such a reputation is particularly important to accounting firms, trust departments, investment advisers, universities, and other organizations that require the public's confidence.

Uniqueness Xerox is unique because it has a process that is protected by patents and no other firm can do quite the same thing. Geographic location is another factor that may affect uniqueness. Tourists flock to Florida beaches in the winter because it is cold up north. Finally, many of these same tourists go to Disney World because there is nothing else like it in the eastern part of the United States.

This list is not exhaustive. It is intended to provide some of the common underpinnings. Others not included in the list are government regulation, taxes, weather, and so on.

Threats

The second part of vulnerability analysis is to determine the threats to the underpinnings of a firm that will occur by a particular date. As previously noted, some of the threats may be observed in the impact matrix. Others are determined by management discussions concerning each of the underpinnings. To demonstrate vulnerability analysis, consider a firm that is evaluating the strategy of entering into the solar-energy field. It will make solar panels that are used to capture sunlight and provide steam-generated electricity.

Table 4-2 shows the major underpinnings of the solar-panel project and the threats that may occur before 1990. The first underpinning—market need—was created by the so-called energy shortage. The principal threats to the energy

Table 4-2 Vulnerability of Solar Panels by 1990

Underpinnings	Threats
1 Market need a Energy shortage	**1** Abundant fuel at relatively low cost **2** Nuclear power

2 Resources
  a Sun
  b Funding
	3 Cloudy weather
	4 Capital shortage
	5 Funds needed elsewhere in firm

3 Customer base
  a Individuals
  b Industry
  c Government
	6 Cost of product is too high relative to competing sources of energy

4 Stable prices a Rising prices on alternate sources of energy	**7** Government subsidy on fuel

5 Technology
  a Storage technology
  b Reflection efficiency
	8 Competing firms develop superior technology first

6 Special abilities a Strong R & D department	No threat
7 Barriers to entry a None	No threat
8 Values—integrity a Public confidence that solar panels are worth the cost	**9** Low-cost competing products that are not cost-effective and give the product a "bad name"
9 Uniqueness a Not applicable	No threat

shortage are that an abundant amount of fuel may be discovered and that the nation will turn increasingly to nuclear power. The second underpinning is resources. In this case, the major natural resource that the solar panels depend on is the sun. The major threat to that resource is an increase in the cloud cover that would make the solar panels ineffective. The firm is also concerned about funding the solar-panel project. The threats to funding it are that there is a capital shortage and that the firm might decide to use its funds on some other projects. The third underpinning concerns the customer base. The customers for the solar panels can include individual households, industry, and government. However, these potential customers will not use solar panels if the cost of the product is too high relative to competing products. The cost includes both the initial cost and the operating cost of the solar panels. The fourth underpinning deals with prices. A basic assumption behind this project is that the cost of competing sources of energy is going to continue to increase over time. However, the government may decide to subsidize some of the energy costs, which would make the solar panels less attractive.

The fifth underpinning—technology—reflects the continued search to improve the quality of the product and expand its uses. However, there is a real threat that other firms will develop superior technology first and gain a dominant share of the market. Nevertheless, it is hoped that the company's strong research and development department (underpinning 6) will develop the new technology first. There are no particular barriers to entry (underpinning 7), but there is some question of integrity (underpinning 8). The public must have confidence in solar panels as a cost-effective source of energy. There is a threat that other firms will sell inferior-quality products that are not cost-effective and give the product a bad name.

Probability and Impact

The final step in the vulnerability analysis is to determine the likelihood that each of the threats will occur by a particular date and the impact of that occurrence on the firm or product. Again, these judgments are made by management. Figure 4-3 is a graphic presentation of the probabilities of the threats that were just discussed and their potential impact on the firm. The numbers shown in Figure 4-3 correspond to the numbered threats listed in Table 4-2. The impacts listed on the vertical axis range from no impact to a catastrophic impact. For example, if threat 1—abundant alternative fuel sources at relatively low cost—occurred, it would have a catastrophic impact because there would be no need for solar panels to provide energy. However, the probability that an abundant low-cost alternative source of energy will be found is very small. Threat 2—nuclear power—will have a strong impact on the firm, and there is a high probability that nuclear power will be developed. The management believes that the cost of the nuclear power will be sufficiently high so that solar panels will still be an attractive source of energy. Threat 3 concerns cloudy weather. The best

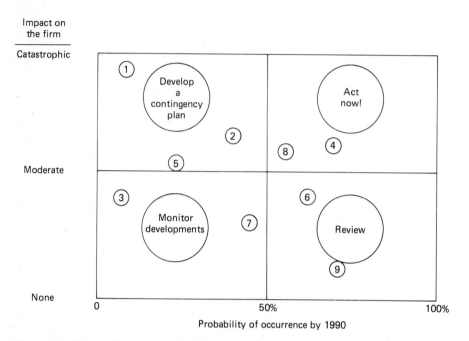

Figure 4-3 Vulnerability matrix. Circled numbers correspond to threats shown in Table 4-2.

weather conditions for the use of solar panels are found in the southern part of the United States where there is ample sunlight and relatively few overcast days. A related problem is that increasing urbanization has resulted in smog that acts like a sun screen and reduces the effectiveness of solar panels. However, new technology directed at increasing the efficiency and storage capacity of solar panels may more than offset the adverse climatic conditions. Like threats 1 to 3, the remaining threats are plotted in the figure to show the likelihood of their occurrence and their impact on the firm.

The vulnerability matrix shown in Figure 4-3 is divided into four quadrants. Threats falling in the upper right-hand quadrant deserve the immediate attention of management because there is a high probability that they will occur and they have a large impact on the firm. Threats 8 and 4 fall into this category. Threat 8 is that competing firms may develop superior technology first. In order to reduce the chances of this happening, the firm can put added emphasis on its own research and development program. Threat 4 concerns an impending capital shortage. In this case the firm can obtain the capital now that it will need for the next few years in order to avoid the capital squeeze in the future. The fact that management is aware of the threats and their impact permits them to take the appropriate action.

The appropriate action for the threats in the upper left quadrant is to develop a contingency plan. The contingency plan permits management to shorten the reaction time if low-cost fuel becomes available (threat 1), if the use of nuclear power becomes widespread (threat 2), and if the firm decides to allocate funds elsewhere in the company (threat 5). The threats that appear in the lower left quadrant should be monitored and those in the lower right quadrant should be reviewed continuously.

In summary, vulnerability analysis provides management with another tool for assessing the impact of threats on their firm. In this case, the threats are aimed at the underpinnings of the business. Once the threats are known and their impact weighed, management can decide what to do about them. The firm evaluating the solar panels decided that there was a good market potential for the product. The threats that were identified for immediate action required some internal decisions. The impact of these threats on the firm is examined next.

ORGANIZATIONAL RESPONSE TO CHANGE

Once particular threats and opportunities that require management action have been identified, management must determine how much effort and resources are required to respond to the threats or to take advantage of the opportunities. The first step in the process of determining the organizational response to change is to identify the functional areas of the firm and the resources that will be required to cope with *each* threat or opportunity. For example, the solar-panel project affects the following functional areas of the company:

A.	Administration	*E.*	Marketing
B.	Financial	*F.*	Personnel
C.	Legal	*G.*	Production
D.	Logistics	*H.*	Research and development

The magnitude of the effort or resources required in each of the functional areas can be measured on a scale of 1 to 5. The magnitudes, like the impacts in the other techniques examined in this chapter, are assigned on the basis of sound judgment by management. As shown below, 1 indicates that a minimal effort is required by the firm. At the other end of the scale, a 5 indicates that a great deal of effort or resources are required.

		Scale		
1	2	3	4	5
Little effort or resources		Moderate effort or resources		Maximum effort or resources

The manufacturer of solar panels used this technique in the following way. The numbers shown below represent the magnitude of effort or resources required in each of the functional areas.

A.	Administration	2	E.	Marketing	3
B.	Financial	4	F.	Personnel	2
C.	Legal	1	G.	Production	3
D.	Logistics	1	H.	Research and development	

These magnitudes are depicted graphically in Figure 4-4. The figure consists of five circles numbered 1 through 5 to represent the scale of magnitudes. The axis *A* through *H* represents the functional areas. The figure that is generated by plotting the magnitudes for each of the functional areas is called a *snowflake diagram* because of its shape. A small snowflake suggests that relatively little effort or resources are required to cope with a particular threat or opportunity, while a large snowflake suggests the opposite. The figure shows that developing the solar panels will require a major research effort (*H*) and substantial financial backing. Although the strategy may be worthwhile, the company decided not to

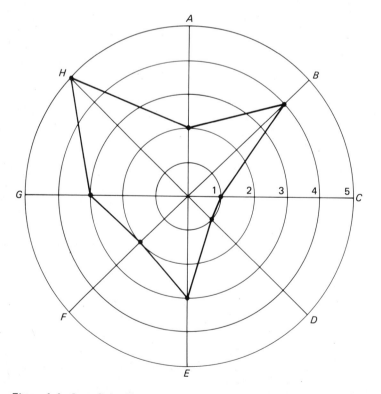

Figure 4-4 Snowflake diagram.

go ahead with it because of prior research and development commitments and because it was not willing to divert the funds necessary to finance this project. Thus the snowflake diagram pointed out some internal constraints that were not obvious when the strategy was evaluated.

CONCLUSION

The external environment (everything that is outside the firm) is one of the most important influences on the growth of business concerns. The factors in external environment can be classified into five categories: economic, physical, political, social, and technological factors. These categories provide a convenient way to monitor the external environment. However, merely monitoring the external environment is not sufficient. It is necessary to determine the impact of the external environment on the firm. This chapter examined three techniques to do just that. The first technique, called an "impact matrix," examines the impacts of trends, events, and the demands of constituents on a firm's missions and strategies. The impacts are based on managerial judgments. Therefore, it is not a precise tool. Unfortunately, there are no tools to measure impacts precisely. Consequently, one uses what is available, recognizing that some information is better than none. An additional benefit of this and the other techniques is that the exercise itself forces management to view strategies and missions from many different perspectives, which may provide useful insights into threats and opportunities.

Vulnerability analysis is the second technique. This technique determines how susceptible an organization is to threats. Specifically, it focuses on the threats to the underpinnings of a business concern or a particular project. Then the likelihood that those threats will occur and their potential impact on the firm are presented in graphic form. The positioning of the threats on the graph indicates the action that is required by the firm.

The snowflake diagram is the third technique that was presented. This technique is useful in assessing management's ability to respond to particular threats or opportunities. In the example presented in connection with the snowflake diagram, the firm that was evaluating solar panels had a good market potential but was unable or unwilling to commit the resources to enter the field.

QUESTIONS[†]

1 What is the economic outlook for the next 6 months? Is it a threat or an opportunity?
2 Assume that you are the manager of a company that produces facial soap products. Explain the impact of each of the following on your firm.
   a The trend of increasing consumerism—demanding more truth in advertising.

[†]Selected solutions at end of book.

   b Demographic factors.
   c Ethnic pride.
   d A newspaper and magazine strike.
   e Higher wages for employees.
3 Assume that your firm has two strategies. Strategy 1 is to sell soaps to non-whites and strategy 2 is to sell to whites. Develop an impact matrix for the items listed in question 2 and the two strategies.
4 Use the following underpinnings and develop a vulnerability matrix for the soap firm. The underpinnings are:
   a Market need.
   b Customer base.
   c Values and integrity.
   d Uniqueness.
5 If you wanted to analyze the market for the soap products in California, what statistical sources would you use?

BIBLIOGRAPHY

Harman, Willis W. *An Incomplete Guide to the Future*. San Francisco, Calif.: San Francisco Book Company, Inc., 1976.

Jain, Subhash, and Surendra Singhvi, eds. *Essentials of Corporate Planning*. Oxford, Ohio: Planning Executives Institute, 1973.

Kahn, Herman, William Brown, and Leon Martel. *The Next 200 Years*. New York: William Morrow & Company, Inc., 1976.

Toffler, Alvin. *Future Shock*. New York: Random House, Inc., 1970.

APPENDIX 4A: Selected Sources of Statistical Data from Federal and State Governments

The following sources may be useful in providing information about the external environment.

United States Government
Agriculture, Census of. Quinquennial (published for years ending in 2 and 7). U.S. Department of Commerce, Washington, D.C. 20233.
Business Conditions Digest. U.S. Department of Commerce.
Business Statistics. U.S. Department of Commerce.
Commodity Situation Reports. U.S. Department of Agriculture, Washington, D.C. 20250.
Construction: Current Reports. U.S. Department of Commerce.
Consumer Price Index: Bureau of Labor Statistics, U.S. Department of Labor, Washington, D.C. 20212.
County and City Data Book. Published after each decennial and quinquennial economic census. U.S. Department of Commerce.

County Business Patterns. Annual. U.S. Department of Commerce.

Economic Indicators. Monthly. Joint Economic Committee by the Council of Economic Advisers.

Enterprise Statistics. Quinquennial. U.S. Department of Commerce.

Federal Reserve Bulletin. Monthly. Federal Reserve Board, Washington, D.C. 20551.

Foreign Trade. Monthly. U.S. Department of Commerce.

Government, Census of. Quinquennial (published for years ending in 2 and 7). U.S. Department of Commerce.

Government Finances and Employment: Current Reports on. Annual except for the quarterly reports on (1) state and local revenue and (2) construction expenditure of state and local governments. U.S. Department of Commerce.

Highway Statistics. Annual. Federal Highway Administration, U.S. Department of Transportation.

Historical Statistics of the United States, Colonial Times to 1970. U.S. Department of Commerce.

Housing, Census of. Decennial (published for years ending in 0). U.S. Department of Commerce.

Housing: Current Reports. Quarterly. U.S. Department of Commerce.

Industrial Production Index. Monthly. Federal Reserve Board.

Location of Manufacturing Plants by County, Industry and Employment Size. Quinquennial. U.S. Department of Commerce.

Manufactures, Census of. Quinquennial (published in years ending in 2 and 7). U.S. Department of Commerce.

Marketing and Transportation Situation. Quarterly. U.S. Department of Agriculture.

Mineral Industries, Census of. Quinquennial (published for years ending in 2 and 7). Department of Commerce.

Pocket Data Book USA. Biennial (published in odd-number years). U.S. Department of Commerce.

Population, Census of. Decennial (published for years ending in 0). U.S. Department of Commerce.

Population: Current Reports. Monthly, annual, and special reports. U.S. Department of Commerce.

Retail Sales: Current Reports. Monthly, annual, monthly issued 10 days after close of month, detailed monthly, and annual. U.S. Department of Commerce.

Retail Trade: Census of Business. Quinquennial (published for years ending in 2 and 7). U.S. Department of Commerce.

Selected Services Trade: Census of Business. Quinquennial (published for years ending in 2 and 7). U.S. Department of Commerce.

Selected Services Trade: Current Business Reports. Monthly. U.S. Department of Commerce.

Statistical Abstract of the United States. Annual. U.S. Department of Commerce.

Statistics of Income: Individual Income Tax Returns. Annual. Internal Revenue Service, U.S. Department of the Treasury.

Survey of Current Business. Monthly. U.S. Department of Commerce.

Transport Statistics in the U.S. Annual Interstate Commerce Commission, Washington, D.C. 20423.

Transportation, Census of. Quinquennial (published for years ending in 2 and 7). U.S. Department of Commerce.

U.S. Industrial Outlook. Annual. U.S. Department of Commerce.

Vital Statistics of the United States. Annual. Public Health Service, U.S. Department of Health, Education and Welfare, Washington, D.C. 20201.

Wholesale Prices and Price Index. Monthly. Bureau of Labor Statistics, U.S. Department of Labor.

Wholesale Trade: Census of Business. Quinquennial (published for years ending in 2 and 7). U.S. Department of Commerce.

State Government

Economic Abstract of Alabama. University of Alabama Center for Business and Economic Research, University, Ala. 35486.

Alaska Statistical Review. Department of Economic Development, Division of Economic Enterprise, Juneau, Alaska 99801.

Arizona Statistical Review. Valley National Bank, Economic Research Department, P.O. Box 71, Phoenix, Ariz. 85001.

Arkansas Almanac. Arkansas Almanac, Inc., Little Rock, Ark. 72114.

California Statistical Abstract. Department of Finance, Budget Division, Sacramento, Calif. 95801.

Colorado Year Book. State Planning Division, Denver, Colo. 80200.

Connecticut Market Data. Connecticut Development Commission, Hartford, Conn. 06100.

Statistical Abstract for the State of Delaware. Delaware State Planning Office, Dover, Del. 19901.

Florida Statistical Abstract. University of Florida, Bureau of Economic and Business Research, Gainesville, Fla. 32601.

Georgia Statistical Abstract. University of Georgia, Division of Research, College of Business Administration, Athens, Ga. 30602.

The State of Hawaii Data Book, A Statistical Abstract. State of Hawaii Department of Planning and Economic Development, Honolulu, Hawaii 96804.

Idaho Statistical Abstract. University of Idaho, Bureau of Business and Economic Research, Moscow, Idaho 83843.

Statistical Abstract. Office of Planning and Analysis, Bureau of the Budget, 216 E. Monroe St., Springfield, Ill. 62706.

Statistical Abstract of Indiana Counties. Indiana State Chamber of Commerce, Indianapolis, Ind. 46200.

Statistical Profile of Iowa. Iowa Development Commission, Research Division, Des Moines, Iowa 50319.

Kansas Statistical Abstract. University of Kansas, Institute for Social and Environmental Studies, Lawrence, Kan. 66045.

Deskbook of Kentucky Economic Statistics. Department of Economic Development, Frankfort, Ky. 40601.

Statistical Abstract of Louisiana. Louisiana State University, Division of Business and Economic Research, New Orleans, La. 70122.

Maine Economic Data Book. Department of Commerce and Industry, Augusta, Maine 04330.

Maryland Statistical Abstract. Department of Economic and Community Development, Annapolis, Md. 21200.

Fact Book. Department of Commerce and Development, Boston, Mass. 02202.

Michigan Statistical Abstract. Bureau of Business and Economic Research, Michigan State University, Graduate School of Business Administration, Division of Research, East Lansing, Mich. 48823.

Minnesota State Statistical Abstract. Minnesota State Planning Agency, Office of Local and Urban Affairs, Saint Paul, Minn. 55103.

Mississippi Statistical Abstract. State College, College of Business and Industry, Division of Research, Mississippi State, Miss. 39762.

Data for Missouri Counties. University of Missouri, Extension Division, Columbia, Mo. 65201.

Montana Data Book. Montana State Division of Planning and Economic Development, Helena, Mont. 59601.

Nebraska Statistical Handbook. Nebraska Department of Economic Development, Division of Research, Box 94666, Lincoln, Neb. 68509.

Nevada Community Profiles. Department of Economic Development, Carson City, Nev. 89701.

Economic Facts Book. Office of Business Economics, Trenton, N.J. 08625.

New Mexico Statistical Abstract. University of New Mexico, Bureau of Business Research, Albuquerque, N. Mex. 87131.

New York State Statistical Yearbook. Division of Budget, Office of Statistical Coordination, Albany, N.Y. 12207.

North Carolina State Statistical Abstract. Department of Administration, Office of the State Budget and Association for Coordinating Interagency Statistics, Raleigh, N.C. 27601.

North Dakota Growth Indicators. Business and Industrial Development Department, Bismarck, N. Dak. 58501.

Statistical Abstract of Ohio. Department of Development, Economic Research Division, Columbus, Ohio 43215.

Statistical Abstract of Oklahoma. University of Oklahoma, Bureau for Business and Economic Research, Norman, Okla. 73069.

Oregon Economic Statistics. University of Oregon, Bureau of Business and Research, 140 Commonwealth Hall, Eugene, Oreg. 97403.

Pennsylvania Statistical Abstract. Department of Commerce, Bureau of Statistics, Harrisburg, Pa. 17120.

Rhode Island Basic Economic Statistics. Rhode Island Development Council, Providence, R.I. 02903.

South Carolina Statistical Abstract. Budget and Control Board, Division of Research and Statistical Services, Columbia, S.C. 29201.

South Dakota Economic and Business Abstract. University of South Dakota, Business Research Bureau, Vermillion, S. Dak. 57069.

Tennessee Statistical Abstract. University of Tennessee, Center for Business and Economic Research, Knoxville, Tenn. 37916.

Texas Almanac. Dallas Morning News, Dallas, Tex. 75201.

Statistical Abstract. University of Utah, Bureau of Economic and Business Research, Salt Lake City, Utah 84112.

Vermont Facts and Figures. Department of Budget and Management, Montpelier, Vt. 05602.

The Research Council's Handbook. Washington State Research Council, Olympia, Wash. 98504.

The Statistical Handbook. West Virginia Research League, Inc., Charleston, W. Va. 25414.

Wisconsin Statistical Abstract. Department of Administration, Information Systems Unit, 1 West Wilson St., Madison, Wis. 53702.

Wyoming Data Book. University of Wyoming, Division of Business and Economic Research, Laramie, Wyo. 82070.

APPENDIX 4B: Selected Sources for United States Market Statistics

"Market Guide." *Editor and Publisher*. Annual. Statistics for states, counties, cities, and SMSAs, including population, personal income, households, farm products, and sales for nine retail-store groups.

A Guide to Consumer Markets. Annual. Statistics and graphs on consumers and their behavior in the marketplace. Sections cover population, employment, income, expenditures, production and distribution, and prices.

Rand McNally Commercial Atlas & Marketing Guide. Annual. Marketing data include basic census data, retail trade volume, auto registrations, etc., for each state by counties, SMSAs, and cities.

"Survey of Buying Power." *Sales and Marketing Management*. Annual, two parts, July and October. Part I: estimates for population, effective buying income and retail sales, for United States and Canadian markets. Part II: survey of media advertising markets, sales by merchandise line for metropolitan areas, and projection figures by market.

"Survey of Industrial Purchasing Power." *Sales and Marketing Management*. Annual, April. Manufacturing production volumes, shipments, employment, purchases, advertising by geographical and industrial divisions, designed to provide indicators of buying potential at various market levels.

Standard Rate & Data Service. Three of the monthly sections (those covering newspapers, spot radio, television) include "Market Data Summary" estimates and SMSA rankings for population, households, consumer spendable income, retail sales by store groups, etc. State, county, and metropolitan-area data also appear at the beginning of the section for each state.

"Statistical & Marketing Report." *Merchandising Week*. Annual, January or February. Tables reviewing sales and retail value, saturation levels, and replacement and trade-in statistics for various selected types of products. Data focused on electronic equipment, and major and minor home appliances, with regional, national, and international reports.

Predicasts. A quarterly service that is especially valuable for market research, providing in one place forecasts from different sources, an index to the articles from which the projections are extracted, and composite forecasts compiled by a major business and economic research staff.

APPENDIX 4C: Sources for United States Financial and Operating Ratios

General

Barometer of Small Business. Accounting Corporation of America. Semiannual. Operating ratios for about 50 retail and service businesses, by sales-volume groups. Tabulated from account books of clients.

Cost of Doing Business in 185 Lines. Dun & Bradstreet, Inc. Biennial. Operating ratios for many retailing, wholesaling, manufacturing lines, as well as for construction, service, transportation, communication, agriculture, and mining.

Key Business Ratios in 125 Lines. Dun & Bradstreet, Inc. Annual. Financial ratios for 125 retailing, wholesaling, manufacturing, construction lines.

Annual Statement Studies. Robert Morris Associates. Financial and operating ratios for over 225 lines of business—manufacturers, wholesalers, retailers, services. Data are broken down by asset size.

Almanac of Business and Industrial Financial Ratios. Leo Troy. Prentice-Hall. Annual. Financial ratios for mining, manufacturing, service, and retail-trade industries shown in each group by size of assets. Taken from the latest Internal Revenue Service data.

Ratios for Specific Industries

Department stores	*Comparative Financial Data, Major Department Stores and Other Leading Merchandisers*. Harris Trust and Savings Bank. Annual.
Distributors	"Annual Survey of Distributor Operations." *Industrial Distribution*. March issue each year.
Food stores	"Annual Report of the Grocery Industry." *Progressive Grocer*. April issue each year. Includes some operating ratios.
Gas companies	*Gas Facts*. American Gas Association. Annual. Includes financial and operating ratios.
Hotels and motels	*Trends in the Hotel-Motel Business*. Harris, Kerr, Forster & Company. Annual.
	Lodging Industry: Annual Report on Hotel and Motor Hotel Operations, Laventhol, Krekstein, Horwath & Horwath. Annual.
	Worldwide Operating Statistics of the Hotel Industry. Horwath & Horwath International and Laventhol, Krekstein, Horwath & Horwath.

Chapter 5

Financial Analysis

Part of the process of introspection consists of financial analysis of the balance sheet, statement of earnings, and statement of changes in financial position, in order to determine strengths or weaknesses and trends. Financial analysis is also used to determine the intrinsic value of a company and for many other purposes. This chapter is concerned with financial analysis as a management tool for assessing present condition. The financial statements of The Jeremy Companies, a hypothetical firm engaged in a wide variety of business activities, are used for purposes of illustration. Three approaches presented here are ratio analysis, percentage analysis, and analysis of the sources and uses of funds.

RATIOS

The balance sheet and statement of earnings for The Jeremy Companies for two consecutive years are shown in Tables 5-1 and 5-2. As each of the ratios is discussed, the appropriate numbers for each calculation are taken from these two financial exhibits. When the ratios require data for 3 years, the data are provided, but the third financial statement is not shown. Many firms use 5 years or

Table 5-1 The Jeremy Companies. Balance Sheets for Years Ended June 30, 1997, and 1996

	1997	1996
Assets		
Current Assets:		
Cash	$ 39,756	$ 16,381
Short-term investments	11,929	—
Accounts receivable	107,042	98,923
Inventory	142,522	146,410
Prepaid expenses	1,646	1,541
Total Current Assets	302,895	263,255
Property and Equipment: at cost		
Land	4,004	3,996
Buildings	50,774	49,631
Equipment	118,345	110,047
Less Depreciation	72,716	68,379
Net Property and Equipment	100,407	95,295
Investments and Other Assets:	8,776	9,161
Total Assets	$412,078	$367,711
Liabilities and Stockholders' Equity		
Current Liabilities		
Accounts Payable	$ 12,017	$ 6,026
Notes Payable	31,085	29,676
Accrued Expenses	59,887	44,248
Income Taxes	18,560	14,335
Total Current Liabilities	121,549	94,285
Long-term debt	41,696	50,931
Other Noncurrent Liabilities	15,193	15,121
Total Liabilities	178,438	160,337
Stockholders' Equity		
Common Stock†	18,986	18,949
Additional Paid-in Capital	46,701	44,985
Retained Earnings	168,152	143,786
	233,839	207,720
Less treasury stock	199	346
Total Equity	233,640	207,374
Total Liabilities and Stockholders' Equity	$412,078	$367,711

†The average number of shares outstanding was 7833 in 1997 and 7714 in 1996.

**Table 5-2   The Jeremy Companies. Statement of Earnings
for Years Ended June 30, 1997, and 1996**

	1997	1996
Net sales	$616,644	$547,733
Cost and expenses:		
Cost of sales	436,248	395,762
Selling, general, operating, and administrative expenses	115,256	99,478
Interest expense	4,481	6,121
Total	555,985	501,361
Earnings before income taxes	60,659	46,372
Provision for other taxes	29,327	21,842
Net earnings	$ 31,332	$ 24,530
Cash dividends	$ 6,966	$ 6,013

more as a basis for their financial analysis. Some financial trends can be detected only over a longer time span. However, the emphasis here is to determine the financial condition of the firm *now* in order to determine its existing strengths and weaknesses. For example, the analysis may reveal the firm is too heavily in debt now. If that is so, how will it finance its long-term capital expansions?

Financial ratios are grouped into four broad categories: (1) profitability, (2) liquidity, (3) efficiency, and (4) financial leverage. Each of these categories contains ratios that provide clues about a company's financial strength that should be thought of as diagnostic tests. A single ratio or diagnostic test does not provide sufficient information about the company to evaluate its current condition. Therefore, several ratios must be used to obtain an overall perspective. Accordingly, a summary of all the ratios that will be discussed is presented at the end of this section (Table 5-3).

Most of the financial ratios that are presented are compared with industry averages to provide a frame of reference. This does not imply that the industry average is the desired standard. It is just a benchmark. Keep in mind that an average is a middle value and that, by definition, half of the firms are above the industry average and half are below it. The important issue is how much deviation from the average is significant to this company.

One reason for deviations from the industry average concerns the phase of development in the product life cycle that was examined in Chapter 2. Figure 5-1 illustrates the product life cycle and provides some generalizations about the financial ratios. For example, during the pioneering phase, there are losses as new products are introduced, the liquidity is low, and the financial leverage is high. In contrast, during the stabilization phase, there are profits, liquidity is increasing, and financial leverage is decreasing. Keep in mind that these are generalizations and that the financial patterns of many firms may differ from those described here. The point is that the level of financial ratios is influenced

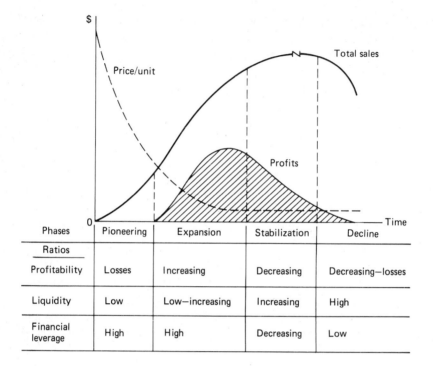

Figure 5-1   The product life cycle and selected financial ratios.

Phases	Pioneering	Expansion	Stabilization	Decline
Ratios				
Profitability	Losses	Increasing	Decreasing	Decreasing—losses
Liquidity	Low	Low—increasing	Increasing	High
Financial leverage	High	High	Decreasing	Low

by the position of the company on the product life cycle as well as by other factors.

Profitability

Profits are the principal test of management's effectiveness. Therefore, they are the first indicator of the condition of the firm. Profitability can be measured in a variety of ways.

Earnings per share is the statistic dealing with profitability that is quoted most often. It is calculated by dividing the earnings available for common stockholders by the average number of shares outstanding. The data show that the earnings per share increased significantly.

1   Earnings per share $= \dfrac{\text{earnings available for common stockholders}}{\text{average number of shares outstanding}}$

$$1997 \quad = \frac{\$31,332}{7,833} = \$4.00$$

$$1996 \quad = \frac{\$24,530}{7,714} = \$3.18$$

Before we continue the discussion of profitability, the way that this ratio is calculated has some very important implications. The numerator—earnings—

of the ratio is taken from the statement of earnings, which is a "flow" statement. That means that the earnings are produced over the period of time. The denominator—the average number of shares—is taken from the balance sheet, which is a "stock" statement that represents one day, June 30. In order to equate the two time periods, the *average* of two balance-sheet dates which cover the same time span as the statement of earnings is used. This concept is simple and should be used *every time* ratios are calculated that involve stocks and flows. However, most textbooks in finance and investments do not use this method consistently.[1] They generally select data from the latest balance-sheet date as being the correct number to use in the equation. The result is that when there are large increases or decreases in balance-sheet items, the resulting ratio will be misleading. For example, the average number of shares outstanding in 1997 was 7833, but 10,000 shares were outstanding at the end of that fiscal year. Using data from only one balance-sheet date for the computation, the earnings per share were $3.13 compared with $4.00 when using the "average" number of shares outstanding. The remaining ratios that are computed with "average" balance-sheet data are marked with an asterisk * in order to draw your attention to them. It should be pointed out that the method of selecting one date for the data from the balance sheet is correct, although the results can be misleading at times. The distinction that is being made here is between being basically correct and being precise.[2]

Now, back to earnings. Earnings can be retained by the company or paid out in the form of cash dividends. If they are retained, the assets of the company will grow at a faster pace than if they are paid out. The subject of financial strategies and dividend policy is discussed in detail in Chapter 7.

The extent to which companies pay dividends is measured by the *payout ratio*, which is the proportion of earnings paid out in the form of cash dividends to the holders of common stock. It can be measured on a per-share basis.

$$\textbf{2} \quad \text{Payout ratio} = \frac{\text{dividends per share}}{\text{earnings per share}}$$

$$1997 \quad = \frac{\$0.89}{\$4.00} = 22.25\%$$

$$1996 \quad = \frac{\$0.78}{\$3.18} = 24.53\%$$

$$\text{Industry average} \quad = 23.06\%$$

[1]Eugene F. Brigham, *Financial Management: Theory and Practice*. Hinsdale, Ill.: The Dryden Press, Inc., 1979, chap. 6.

Lawrence J. Gitman, *Principles of Managerial Finance*, 2d ed. New York, Harper & Row, Publishers, Incorporated, 1979, chap. 3.

Erich A. Helfret, *Techniques of Financial Analysis*, 4th ed. Homewood, Ill.: Richard D. Irwin, Inc., 1977, chap. 2.

James C. Van Horne, *Financial Management and Policy*, 4th ed. Englewood Cliffs, N.J.: Prentice-Hall, Inc., 1977, chap. 25.

[2]The author is particularly indebted to Dr. Linda Mitchusson, Professor of Accounting, Wichita State University, who pointed out the distinction between "being basically correct and being precise."

Corporations in the United States generally pay out between 40 and 50 percent of their after-tax profits in the form of cash dividends. However, the payout ratios for both, The Jeremy Companies and the industry, are substantially below that figure. One reason is that firms in this industry are growing rapidly and require substantial funds to support their growth. Therefore, they retain most of their earnings.

Profitability can also be measured in terms of returns on sales, assets, and equity. The *profit margin* on sales is computed by dividing net profits after taxes by net sales. The profit margin is the percent profit earned for each dollar of sales. The profit margin for The Jeremy Companies improved in the most recent year but is still somewhat below the industry average.

$$\textbf{3} \quad \text{Profit margin} = \frac{\text{net profit after taxes}}{\text{net sales}}$$

$$1997 \quad = \frac{\$31,332}{616,644} = 5.08\%$$

$$1996 \quad = \frac{\$24,530}{547,733} = 4.48\%$$

Industry average $\quad = 5.25\%$

Return on total assets measures the productivity of assets for stockholders, bondholders, and other creditors. It is calculated by dividing earnings before interest and taxes by average assets. The ratio reflects the return on average total assets without any consideration of how those assets were financed. Frequently net profits after taxes plus interest is used as the numerator of this ratio. However, this method reflects the influence of debt financing because the income tax computation takes into account the tax deduction for interest. The data for The Jeremy Companies show a marked improvement in the return on assets. In the most recent year, the return was consistent with the industry average.

$$\textbf{*4} \quad \text{Return on assets} = \frac{\text{earnings before interest and taxes}}{\text{average total assets}}$$

$$1997 \quad = \frac{\$60,659 + \$4,481}{(\$412,078 + \$367,711)/2} = 16.71\%$$

$$1996^{\dagger} \quad = \frac{\$46,372 + \$6,121}{\$355,230} = 14.78\%$$

Industry average $\quad = 16.62\%$

†Because data for 1995 are now shown in the financial statements, the "average" total assets for 1996 are presented without showing the computation.

Rate of return on equity measures the rate of return on the owners' investment and is calculated by dividing net profits after taxes by the average total stockholders' equity. When large amounts of preferred stock are outstanding, a similar ratio can be computed by dividing income available to common equity by common equity. There are no preferred shares at The Jeremy Companies. Therefore, the former ratio was used. The data show that the companies' ratio is improving and is above average in the latest year.

---

*5 Rate of return on equity $= \dfrac{\text{net profits after taxes}}{\text{average total stockholders' equity}}$

$$1997 = \frac{\$31,332}{\$220,507} = 14.21\%$$

$$1996 = \frac{\$24,530}{\$191,365} = 12.82\%$$

Industry average $= 13.01\%$

Liquidity

A company must survive the short run in order to prosper in the long run. The following indicators are concerned with a company's ability to meet its short-term or current obligations, which are those that are due within 1 year. Generally, such obligations are paid off by reducing current assets, which are those that can be converted into cash on relatively short notice. The difference between the current assets and current liabilities is commonly called *net working capital*. It represents the amount remaining after all the current obligations have been accounted for. An examination of The Jeremy Companies' balance sheet reveals that the net working capital increased from $168,970 in 1996 to $181,346 in 1997.

---

6 Net working capital = current assets − current liabilities

1997   = \$302,895 − \$121,549 = \$181,346

1996   = \$263,255 − \$ 94,285 = \$168,970

The current ratio is a broad measure of liquidity and is computed by dividing current assets by current liabilities. The industry average is 2.00 times, which means that the current assets were twice as large as the liabilities. The current ratio for The Jeremy Companies was substantially above the industry average in 1996, and then declined somewhat in the following year. Nevertheless, it was still relatively high. A high current ratio may be a warning flag suggesting that the firm is not using its current assets efficiently. On the other hand, the firm may be building liquidity because of uncertain economic conditions in the future or in order to buy another company. In either case, an extremely high or low ratio merits further investigation.

7   Current ratio = $\dfrac{\text{current assets}}{\text{current liabilities}}$

   1997 $= \dfrac{\$302,895}{\$121,549} = 2.49\text{X}$ (X = times)

   1996 $= \dfrac{\$263,255}{\$\ 94,285} = 2.79\text{X}$

   Industry average $= 2.00\text{X}$

The *acid-test ratio* is derived by dividing cash, marketable securites, and net accounts receivable by current liabilities. This ratio gives a "narrow" perspective of liquidity because it excludes the least liquid current assets—inventories and prepaid items. The acid-test ratio for The Jeremy Companies was substantially above the industry average in both years. Collectively, the three measures of liquidity (net working capital, current ratio, acid-test ratio) suggest that the company may have more liquidity than it needs. Although liquidity may be desirable, excess liquidity can have an adverse effect on profitability.

8   Acid-test ratio = $\dfrac{\text{cash + marketable securities + accounts receivable}}{\text{current liabilities}}$

   1997 $= \dfrac{\$39,756 + 11,929 + 107,042}{\$121,549} = 1.31\text{X}$

   1996 $= \dfrac{\$16,381 + 98,923}{\$94,285} = 1.22\text{X}$

   Industry average $= 1.05\text{X}$

Efficiency Ratios

Efficiency ratios are sometimes called activity ratios. They measure how actively certain assets are being used, and this is a clue to their efficiency. For example, the faster inventories are turned over (sold) and the faster accounts receivable are collected, the more money will be available for expansion, expenses, and profits.

The *inventory turnover ratio* measures how many times the inventory is sold or turned over each year. It is calculated by dividing the cost of sales by average inventory. The inventory turnover ratio will vary widely from industry to industry. The inventory turnover ratio for a newsstand should be very high (365X would be the maximum ratio), while the turnover ratio for a retail jewelry store may be low (2X to 3X). The ratios for The Jeremy Companies suggest that it is in one of the industries where the turnover ratio is low. Nevertheless, inventory turnover for The Jeremy Company is somewhat below that of the industry, but it is improving.

---

*9 Inventory turnover ratio = $\dfrac{\text{cost of sales}}{\text{average inventory}}$

$$1997 \quad = \frac{\$436,248}{\$144,466} = 3.02\times$$

$$1996 \quad = \frac{\$395,762}{\$140,210} = 2.82\times$$

Industry average $= 3.10\times$

The *average collection period* of accounts receivable measures the number of days' sales that are tied up in receivables. It indicates the average length of time that a firm must wait before receiving cash for sales that were made on credit. Two methods for calculating the ratio are presented here. The first method is to divide the average accounts receivable by net sales and multiply the resulting number by 360 days. Most financial analysts use 360 days rather than 365 days to calculate this and other ratios. This method of calculating the ratio reveals the average collection period is 60 days.

---

*10a Average collection period = $\dfrac{\text{average accounts receivable} \times 360}{\text{net sales}}$

$$1997 \quad = \frac{\$102,983}{\$616,644} \times 360$$

$$= 0.167 \times 360 = 60.12 \text{ days}$$

The second method of calculating the ratio consists of two steps. The first step is to determine the average sales per day. This is accomplished by dividing net sales by 360. The next step is to divide the average accounts receivable by average sales per day. This method reveals average sales per day and the average collection period. The data reveal that the average collection period is longer than the industry average. In other words, their collections are slow.

---

*10b Average collection period = (a) $\dfrac{\text{net sales}}{360 \text{ days}}$ = average sales per day

(b) $\dfrac{\text{average accounts receivable}}{\text{average sales per day}}$

$$1997 \quad = (a) \; \$616,644 = \$1,713 \text{ average sales per day}$$

$$(b) \; \frac{\$102,983}{\$ \; 1,713} = 60.12 \text{ days}$$

$$1996 \quad = (a) \; \frac{\$547,733}{360} = \$1,521 \text{ average sales per day}$$

$$(b) \; \frac{\$95,631}{\$ \; 1,521} = 62.87 \text{ days}$$

Industry average $= 58.75 \text{ days}$

Fixed-asset turnover is the ratio of net sales to average fixed assets, and it indicates how efficiently the fixed assets are being used. On balance, the ratios for The Jeremy Companies are comparable with the industry averages.

---

*11 Fixed-asset turnover $= \dfrac{\text{net sales}}{\text{average total fixed assets}}$

$$1997 \quad = \dfrac{\$616,644}{\$\ 97,851} = 6.30\times$$

$$1996 \quad = \dfrac{\$547,733}{\$\ 90,055} = 6.08\times$$

Industry average $\qquad\qquad = 6.20\times$

In summary, the "efficiency" ratios indicate The Jeremy Companies are less efficient than the industry average. Most of the slack appears to be in the management of current assets—inventory and collections. Stated otherwise, they are less efficient than the "average." However, the word "average" means middle or median value. By definition, one half of the firms are above average and one half are below average. Therefore, being below average is not necessarily bad. The important issue is how far below average is considered bad.

Financial Leverage

Financial leverage refers to the relationship between fixed debt obligations, such as bonds, mortgages, and leases, and common stockholders' equity. Some analysts include preferred stock as a fixed obligation. Companies that have a high proportion of fixed obligations are said to be highly levered. Leverage increases the volatility of earnings per share and the financial risk of the company. More will be said about this in Chapter 10.

Long-term debt expressed as a *percent of total capital* is one indicator of financial leverage. Total capital includes both long-term debt and equity. The data show that The Jeremy Companies reduced their long-term debt in both absolute and relative terms. In the most recent year, the proportion of long-term debt to total capital was significantly below the industry average. However, this may be a part of an effort to restructure their capital and reduce their interest expenses.

---

*12   Long-term debt as percent of total capital

Long-term debt	$\ 41,969 = 15.23\%$	$\ 50,931 = 19.72\%$
Total equity	$233,640	$207,374
Total capital	$275,609	$258,305
Industry average		$= 21.35\%$

By reducing the amount of long-term debt outstanding and increasing earnings, the company has a greater ability to *cover* its fixed charges. Thus it has reduced its financial-leverage risk. The coverage of debt service can be measured by dividing interest charges into earnings before interest and taxes. This ratio indicates that the company's ability to cover or pay its fixed charges improved significantly. If the company had a large amount of preferred stock outstanding, the dividend on the preferred stock could have been included in the denominator of the equation. Strictly speaking, preferred stocks are not a "debt," but they are a fixed obligation of the company. The revised equation would reflect the coverage for all fixed charges on securities. The ratio can also be expanded to include lease payments and other fixed items.

---

13   Debt coverage $= \dfrac{\text{profit before interest and taxes}}{\text{interest expense}}$

1997 $= \dfrac{\$60,659 + \$4,481}{\$4,481} = 14.54\times$

1996 $= \dfrac{\$46,372 + \$6,121}{\$6,121} = 8.58\times$

Industry average $= 7.65\times$

The *cost of long-term debt* is the final ratio to be discussed in connection with financial leverage. The cost is determined by dividing interest expense by average long-term debt. The data show that the reduction in long-term debt eliminated some of the high-cost bonds and lowered the cost of the remaining debt to well below the industry average. Note that the cost is based on the book value of the outstanding debt. Sometimes, the market value of outstanding debt is used.

---

*14   Cost of long-term debt $= \dfrac{\text{interest expense}}{\text{average long-term debt}}$

1997 $= \dfrac{\$\ 4,481}{\$46,314} = 9.67\%$

1996 $= \dfrac{\$\ 6,121}{\$53,612} = 11.42\%$

Industry average $= 10.80\%$

Review of Indicators

Table 5-3 lists the indicators that were presented in this section. The major items that stand out are that The Jeremy Companies appear to have excess liquidity and are not using their assets efficiently. Profitability could be improved by increasing their efficiency ratios and making greater use of financial leverage.

Table 5-3 Summary of Financial Indicators for The Jeremy Companies

Ratio or indicator	Formula	Results		Industry average	Evaluation
		1997	1996		
Profitability					
*1 Earnings per share	Earnings available for common stockholders / Average number of shares outstanding	$4.00	$3.18		
2 Payout ratio	Dividends per share / Earnings per share	22.25%	24.53%	23.06%	Fair
3 Profit margin	Net profit after taxes / Net sales	5.08%	4.48%	5.25%	Slightly low
*4 Return on assets	Earnings before interest and taxes / Average total assets	16.71%	14.78%	16.62%	Average
*5 Rate of return on equity	Net profit after taxes / Average total stockholders' equity	14.21%	12.82%	13.01%	Above average
Liquidity					
6 Net working capital	Current assets − current liabilities	$181,316	$168,970		
7 Current ratio	Current assets / Current liabilities	2.49X	2.79X	2.00X	Too high?
8 Acid-test ratio	Cash + marketable securities + receivables / Current liabilities	1.31X	1.22X	1.05X	Too high

Table 5-3 Summary of Financial Indicators for The Jeremy Companies (*Continued*)

Ratio or indicator	Formula	Results 1997	Results 1996	Industry average	Evaluation
Efficiency					
*9 Inventory turnover ratio	$\dfrac{\text{Cost of sales}}{\text{Average inventory}}$	3.02X	2.82X	3.10X	Somewhat low
*10 Average collection period	$\dfrac{\text{Net sales}}{360}$ = Average sales per day $1713	$1713	$1,521		
	$\dfrac{\text{Average accounts receivable}}{\text{Average sales per day}}$	60.12 days	62.87 days	58.75 days	Slow collection
*11 Fixed-asset turnover	$\dfrac{\text{Net sales}}{\text{Average total fixed assets}}$	6.30X	6.08X	6.20X	Satisfactory
Financial leverage					
12 Long-term debt as percent of total capital	$\dfrac{\text{Long-term debt}}{\text{Total capital}}$	15.23%	19.72%	21.35%	Low
13 Debt coverage	$\dfrac{\text{Profits before interest and taxes}}{\text{Interest}}$	14.54X	8.58X	7.65X	Very good
*14 Cost of long-term debt	$\dfrac{\text{Interest}}{\text{Average long-term debt}}$	9.67%	11.42%	10.80%	Very good

*Denotes average balance-sheet value was used in computation.

x = times.

PERCENT INCOME STATEMENT

The percent income statement expresses all the items listed in the income statement as a percent of net sales (see Table 5-4). This method puts everything on a relative basis and is useful in pinpointing changes in the composition of earnings and expenses. The percent income statement for The Jeremy Companies shows that the cost of sales was relatively less in 1997 than in the previous year. However, the reduction in the cost of interest was more than offset by relatively higher expenses for selling, operations, and administration. Nevertheless, earnings before and after taxes improved markedly. The technique of putting every item on a percentage basis can also be used to compare balance sheets of firms of different asset size.

Before leaving the income statement, it is advisable to analyze the growth of income and sales over time. This is particularly important during inflationary periods. For example, the sales of The Jeremy Companies increased from $547,733 in 1996 to $616,644 in 1997, which is a 12.5 percent increase. If inflation had increased 14 percent during the same period, there would have been a reduction in the *real* level of sales. Stated otherwise, the level of sales in 1997 adjusted for inflation would have declined to $530,276, which is below the previous year's level.

Net sales in 1997	$616,644
Less 14%	86,234
Equals sales adjusted for inflation	$530,276

Finally, income statements can also be viewed in the context of the life cycle. The pattern of sales and revenues is depicted in Figure 5-1. The relationship between costs and the life cycle is explained in Chapter 11.

Table 5-4   The Jeremy Companies. Percent Statement of Earnings[†]

	1997	1996
Net sales	100.00%	100.00%
Cost and expenses:		
Cost of sales	70.75	72.25
Selling, general, operating, and administrative expenses	18.69	18.16
Interest expense	0.73	1.11
Total	90.16	91.53
Earnings before income taxes	9.84	8.47
Provision for other taxes	4.76	3.99
Net earnings	5.08	4.48

†Because of rounding, numbers may not add to totals.

SOURCE AND USE OF FUNDS

The *statement of changes of financial position* shown in Table 5-5 is a useful analytical tool. It lists the major sources and uses of funds and explains the difference by changes in working capital. For example, in 1997, the total resources provided amounted to $45,966, and in the previous year they amounted to $45,507. Because the totals are roughly the same, the compositions of the two amounts are comparable. In 1996, a much larger proportion of the resources

Table 5-5 The Jeremy Companies. Statement of Changes of Financial Position for the Years Ended June 30, 1997, and 1996

	1997 ($000)	1996 ($000)
Resources provided		
Net earnings	$31,332	$24,530
Depreciation and other items not causing changes in working capital	12,760	9,730
Total from operations	44,092	34,260
Sale of property	1,445	253
Sale of common stock	1,250	4,735
Increase (decrease) in other noncurrent liabilities	(821)	6,259
Total resources provided	$45,966	$45,507
Resources applied		
Purchase of equipment	$17,826	$22,270
Retirement of long-term debt	9,235	5,176
Cash dividends declared	6,966	6,013
Other increases (decreases)	(437)	159
Increase in working capital	12,376	11,889
Total resources applied	$45,966	$45,507
Changes in working capital		
Increases (decreases) in current assets		
Cash	$23,375	$ 405
Short-term investments	11,929	
Net accounts receivable	8,119	8,756
Inventories	(3,888)	(6,611)
Prepaid expenses	105	469
Total	$39,640	$ 3,019
Decreases (increases) in current liabilities		
Notes payable	(5,591)	12,485
Accounts payable	(1,409)	3,408
Accrued expenses	(15,639)	(11,239)
Income taxes	(4,225)	4,216
Total	(27,264)	8,870
Increase in working capital	$12,376	$11,889

Table 5-6   Time Required to Obtain Funds

Sources of funds	Time, in months		
	0–6	6–18	18, or more
Cash	X		
Sell marketable securities	X		
Obtain business loan	X		
Sell bonds		X	
Sell stock		X	
Reduce expenses	X	X	
Reduce case dividends	X	X	
Sell real estate			X
Sell other fixed assets			X

was provided by the sale of stock and increases in other noncurrent liabilities than in the following year. In 1997, net earnings accounted for the bulk of the total resources provided.

On the spending side of the equation, there were also marked differences in the application of funds. In 1997, fewer funds were spent for the purchase of equipment, and more were spent on the retirement of debt, increasing dividends and working capital.

The changes in the working capital are particularly interesting. Although the total increase in working capital was not appreciably different in the two years ($12,376 vs. $11,889), the factors that contributed to that total deserve comment. In 1997, there were large increases in current liabilities, whereas there were decreases in the previous year. Most of the increases in the liabilities in 1997 were used to increase cash and short-term investments.

Keep in mind that it may take a substantial amount of time to obtain some sources of funds. As shown in Table 5-6, some sources of funds, such as reductions in cash holdings and the sale of marketable securities, are available immediately. However, one cannot sell corporate securities immediately because it takes time to register the securities with the Securities and Exchange Commission and market conditions may not be favorable for a new securities offering. Similarly, it may take several years to sell a parcel of real estate or some other fixed asset. Thus the time required to obtain funds must be taken into account in the planning process.

CONCLUSION

This chapter explained some of the fundamentals of financial analysis. The first part of the chapter examined financial ratios, which were divided into four categories: profitability, liquidity, efficiency, and financial leverage. Several ratios in each category were discussed, and then all ratios were reviewed. A variety of financial ratios must be used to analyze a company properly. No single ratio by itself is sufficient. Moreover, caution should be used in comparing ratios with industry averages. The term average means a middle value; half of the firms are above average and half are below it. The firm's position on the product life cycle is also an important consideration when interpreting ratios.

The chapter also explained how to use a percent income statement. This tool is particularly effective in tracking trends in revenues and expenses over time. Finally, the statement of changes in financial position was examined; this tool is used to analyze sources and uses of funds and working capital. The point of the entire analysis is to provide a frame of reference for the financial condition of the firm at this time. It is part of the introspection process. The firm must know its current financial strengths and weaknesses for intelligent planning. If the strategic plan calls for large expenditures that will require additional debt and equity financing, it will fail unless the firm is able to obtain the funds. By analyzing its current financial condition, it is possible to determine if the firm is capable of meeting the challenges of the future.

QUESTIONS[†]

1 Why are the concepts "stock" and "flow" important in financial analysis?
2 How can a firm's location on the life cycle be taken into account in financial analysis?
3 Is a rate of return on assets of 19 percent good?
4 What is the meaning of the term "liquidity"?
5 During the introspection of your firm, it was discovered that it will need 50 percent more capital to support projected growth. How can the firm obtain additional capital, and how long will it take?

BIBLIOGRAPHY

Brigham, Eugene F. *Financial Management: Theory and Practice*. Hinsdale, Ill.: The Dryden Press, Inc., 1979.

Foster, George. *Financial Statement Analysis*. Englewood Cliffs, N.J.: Prentice-Hall, Inc., 1978.

Helfret, Erich A. *Techniques of Financial Analysis*, 4th ed. Homewood, Ill.: Richard D. Irwin, Inc., 1977.

Viscone, Jerry A. *Financial Analysis: Principles and Procedures*. Boston, Mass.: Houghton Mifflin Company, 1977.

Weston, Fred J., and Eugene Brigham. *Managerial Finance*, 6th ed. Hinsdale, Ill.: The Dryden Press, Inc., 1978.

[†]Selected solutions at end of book.

Part Three

Financial Decisions

Strategic planning refers to major action programs that are used by an organization to achieve its missions and goals. Strategic planning is making decisions today that will affect the future course of an organization. Successful strategic decisions are those that result in profits—or reduced losses. This part of the book explains how to use certain financial tools to make strategic decisions. Chapter 6 demonstrates several uses of break-even analysis. Chapter 7 is about compound interest, which is the basis of all discounted cash flow techniques. Chapter 8 explains discounted cash flow techniques and how they may be used to make strategic decisions. Chapter 9 is concerned with models. This chapter explains some of the benefits and pitfalls of using models.

Chapter 6

Chapter 6

Break-Even Analysis

The management of Lockheed Aircraft Corporation made a strategic decision to build the L-1011 TriStar, a wide-bodied commercial jet capable of carrying up to 400 passengers. In making this decision, Lockheed's management relied heavily on break-even analysis.[1] The term break-even refers to a level of operations at which the revenues just cover the total costs. Lockheed determined that they had to sell between 195 and 205 L-1011s at about $15 million each to break even on this project. They projected total demand of 775 aircraft of a similar type and assumed that they would obtain a sufficient share of that potential market to make the L-1011 program a viable commercial endeavor.[2]

Break-even analysis is one of several techniques that may be used to

[1]U. E. Reinhardt, "Break-Even Analysis for Lockheed's TriStar: An Application of Financial Theory," *The Journal of Finance*, September 1973, pp. 821–838. This article indicates that although Lockheed's management used break-even analysis, they might have changed their decision to produce the L-1011 if they had used other methods of analysis, such as those explained in Chapter 8.

[2]U.S. Congress, Emergency Loan Guarantee Legislation, Hearings before the Committee on Banking, Housing and Urban Affairs, Senate, Ninety-Second Congress, 1st sess., Part 1, June 7–16, 1971, pp. 224–225.

determine if the strategy to build the L-1101 or any project is economically feasible. Break-even analysis provides information about the number of units that must be sold to break even, the sensitivity of the break-even points to changes in sales price and costs, the amount of revenue that must be obtained to break even, and other factors. Other techniques for making decisions, including net present value and the internal rate of return, are presented in Chapter 8.

PRICES AND COSTS

In order to calculate the break-even point, three simplifying assumptions are made with respect to price and costs. Although the assumptions may seem unrealistic, they permit us to have a common starting point for understanding some of the relationships among costs, volume, and revenues. Then the assumptions can be relaxed in order to make the analysis more realistic.

Price

The first assumption is that the selling price is independent of the number of units sold. This means that the selling price is fixed and cannot be reduced in an effort to stimulate sales. Accordingly, total sales revenues are a fixed percentage of sales; therefore, total revenue appears as a straight line on the break-even chart that is presented shortly. This type of analysis is called linear break-even analysis because it is limited to straight lines.

Fixed Costs

The second assumption is that fixed costs are independent of the number of units sold. Examples of fixed costs include interest on borrowed funds, depreciation on plant and equipment, salaries, and general office expenses. As shown in Figure 6-1, fixed costs are represented by a horizontal line. In this exhibit, the fixed costs are $10,000 whether sales are 0, 100, 200, or 300 units.

Variable Costs

The third assumption is that variable costs change in direct proportion to the number of units sold. Packaging and delivery costs are examples of variable costs. As shown in Figure 6-1, variable costs are represented by a straight line that begins at the origin, and it is positively sloped to the right. When there are no sales, the variable costs are zero. When 100 units are sold, the variable costs are $10,000, and when 200 units are sold, the variable costs are $20,000. Thus variable costs are a fixed percentage of the number of units sold. Frequently, the variable cost per unit is expressed as a dollar amount (e.g., $1.20).

Semivariable Costs

Some costs are neither fish nor fowl. They have characteristics of both fixed and variable costs. For example, sales commissions may be fixed for a certain

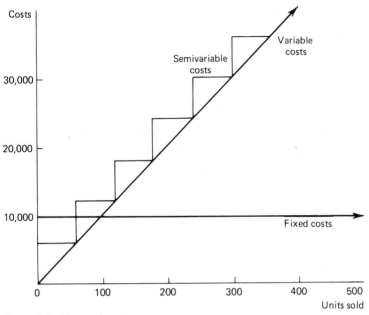

Figure 6-1 Types of costs.

number of units sold, and then be increased for larger volumes of sales. Similarly, telephone expenses are fixed, but when sales increase, more telephones are needed to service the accounts, and telephone expenses increase. Semivariable costs are depicted as steps in Figure 6-1. Now that the basic terms have been defined, we can calculate the break-even point.

CALCULATING THE BREAK-EVEN POINT

Trial and Error

Table 6-1 shows the calculation of a break-even point by using the trial-and-error method. In this example, the selling price is $4 per unit, variable costs are $2 per unit, and fixed costs are $50,000. If 5000 units are sold, the total revenue is $20,000 (5000 × $4 = $20,000). The total costs, $60,000, are determined by adding the variable costs (5000 × $2 = $10,000) to the fixed costs ($50,000). At this level of sales, total costs exceed total revenue by $40,000. The process of calculating revenues and costs is repeated for different levels of sales until total costs are just covered by total revenue. The break-even point is 25,000. When sales exceed 25,000 units, there is a profit, and when sales are less than 25,000 units, there is a loss. At the break-even point, there is neither a profit nor a loss; earnings before interest and taxes (EBIT) are equal to zero. Profit or loss is equal to EBIT.

Table 6-1   Break-Even Point in Units, Using Trial-and-Error Method

Price per unit P (1)	Quantity sold Q (2)	Total revenue R = P · Q (3) = (1) × (2)	Variable costs/unit V (4)	Fixed costs F (5)	Total costs C = V + F (6) = (4) + (5)	Earned before interest and taxes EBIT (7) = (3) − (6)
$4	5,000	$ 20,000	$10,000	$50,000	$ 60,000	$(40,000) ‡
4	10,000	40,000	20,000	50,000	70,000	(30,000)
4	15,000	60,000	30,000	50,000	80,000	(20,000)
4	20,000	80,000	40,000	50,000	90,000	(10,000)
4	25,000	100,000	50,000	50,000	100,000	0
4	30,000	120,000	60,000	50,000	110,000	10,000
4	35,000	140,000	70,000	50,000	120,000	20,000
4	40,000	160,000	80,000	50,000	130,000	30,000
4	45,000	180,000	90,000	50,000	140,000	40,000

†V = $2 per unit.
‡( ) = loss.

Graphic Method

The break-even point also may be determined by using the graphic method. The data presented to Table 6-1 are plotted on the graph shown in Figure 6-2. Although both methods produce the same results, some analysts prefer the graphic

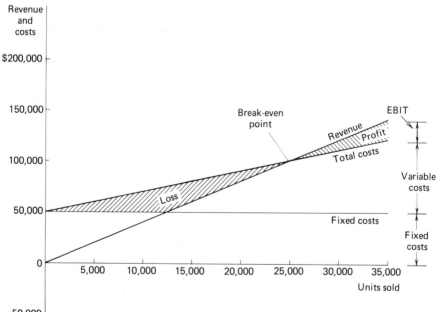

Figure 6-2 Break-even in units graphic method.

method because only a few calculations are required to plot the straight line, and it is easier to make "visual" comparisons of charts than it is to study lengthy tables. In spite of the ease of calculation and interpretation, the graphic method lacks the precision that is available by using the trial-and-error method or the algebraic method.

Algebraic Method

The algebraic method provides a quick and accurate way of determining the break-even point. As in the other methods, one must know the price per unit, total fixed costs, and variable fixed costs. The equation for the break-even point[3] is

$$Q = \frac{F}{P - V} \tag{6-1}$$

where Q = break-even quantity
P = price per unit
F = total fixed costs
V = variable costs per unit

By way of illustration, let's use the same numbers that were used to demonstrate the other two methods. Accordingly,

$F = \$50,000$
$P = \$4$
$V = \$2$

and the algebraic solution to the break-even point is

$$Q = \frac{F}{P - V}$$
$$= \frac{\$50,000}{\$4 - \$2}$$
$$= 25,000 \text{ units}$$

---

[3] At the break-even point total revenue is equal to total cost

$$\begin{aligned}
\text{Total revenue} &= (P \cdot Q) \\
\text{Total cost} &= F + (V \cdot Q) \\
\text{then} \quad (P \cdot Q) &= F + (V \cdot Q) \\
(P \cdot Q) - (V \cdot Q) &= F \\
Q(P - V) &= F \\
Q &= \frac{F}{P - V}
\end{aligned}$$

Table 6-2   Effects on Break-Even Point of Changing Price per Unit and Costs

	Change in		
	Price per unit (+)	Fixed costs (−)	Variable costs (−)
Break-even points in units	−	−	−
EBIT	+	+	+

Note that a decrease (−) in price or an increase (+) in costs will have the opposite impact on the break-even point and EBIT.

Sensitivity

The algebraic method is particularly useful in testing the sensitivity of the break-even points to changes in sales price and costs. The general relationships among revenues, costs, and the break-even point in units and earnings before interest and taxes (EBIT) are shown in Table 6-2. If price per unit increases (+), the break-even point in terms of units will decline (−), and the EBIT will increase (+). Similarly, a reduction in variable costs will lower the break-even point and increase the EBIT. An increase in costs will have the opposite effect on the break-even point and EBIT. For example, assume that a firm is considering raising the price from $4 to $5 per unit and wants to know what impact this action will have on the break-even point. The solution to the problem is

$$Q = \frac{\$50,000}{\$5 - \$2}$$
$$= 16,667 \text{ units}$$

Thus a 25 percent increase in the price (from $4 to $5) per unit resulted in a 33 percent reduction in the break-even point.

Break-Even Revenue

Another way to use break-even analysis is to calculate the break-even revenue (total revenue from sales) instead of the break-even point in terms of units sold. The break-even revenue can be determined by solving Equation (6-2).

$$\text{Break-even revenue} = \frac{F}{1 - V/R} \qquad (6\text{-}2)$$

where F = fixed costs
  V = variable costs
  R = sales revenue

The equation is used in the following manner. Using data from Table 6-1, assume that 5000 units are sold at $4 per unit, the fixed costs are $50,000, and the variable costs are $2 per unit. The break-even revenue[4] is

$$\text{Break-even revenue} = \frac{F}{1 - V/R} \qquad (6\text{-}2)$$

$$= \frac{\$50,000}{1 - \$10,000/\$20,000}$$

$$= \frac{\$50,000}{0.5}$$

$$= \$100,000$$

Equation (6-2) also can be used to test the sensitivity of the break-even revenue to changes in sales price and costs. For example, increasing the price from $4 to $5 per unit lowers the break-even revenue to $83,333, or by 16.7 percent.

Operating Leverage

Operating leverage reflects the extent to which fixed costs affect profits which are earnings before interest and taxes (EBIT). High levels of fixed costs produce high operating leverage, and low levels of fixed costs produce low operating leverage. In order to clarify the impact of fixed costs on EBIT, consider the example presented in Table 6-3. In this example, sales for both the high- and low-operating-leverage firms increased 100 percent. The EBIT of the firm with low operating leverage increased only 112.5 percent. The difference between the two firms is that the firm with high operating leverage has high fixed costs and the firm with low operating leverage has low fixed costs. Therefore, operating leverage is a function of fixed costs.

Operating leverage can be measured by Equation (6-3).

[4] Proof:

Revenue at break-even point = $100,000	
Less variable costs at break-even point	−50,000
Less fixed costs	−50,000
Equals EBIT	$ 0

Table 6-3 Operating Leverage

	High-operating-leverage firm			Low-operating-leverage firm		
	year 1	+100%	year 2	year 1	+100%	year 2
Sales revenue	$1000		$2000	$1000		$2000
less fixed costs	800		800	100		100
less variable costs	100		200	100		200
= EBIT	$ 100		$1000	$ 800		$1700
		+900%			+112.5%	

$$\text{Operating leverage OL} = \frac{\text{percent change in EBIT}}{\text{percent change in sales}} > 1 \qquad (6\text{-}3)$$

This equation shows that operating leverage exists whenever the percentage change in EBIT is greater than the percentage change in sales. Applying the data from Table 6-3 to the equation, the operating leverage for both firms is

$$\text{OL} = \frac{\text{percent change in EBIT}}{\text{percent change in sales}}$$

Firm with high operating leverage $\quad \text{OL} = \dfrac{900 \text{ percent}}{100 \text{ percent}} = 9$

Firm with low operating leverage $\quad \text{OL} = \dfrac{112.5 \text{ percent}}{100 \text{ percent}} = 1.125$

This method provides additional insight into operating leverage, but it should be used with caution when comparing the ratios for two or more firms. The comparison will not be valid unless the level of sales used for both firms is the same. This is so because the degree of operating leverage depends, in part, on the base level of sales. In addition, if the firm is close to its break-even point, changes in sales will have a particularly dramatic impact on the percentage change in EBIT. Keep in mind that the EBIT at the break-even point is zero, so that any increases in revenue from that low level will result in large percentage changes in EBIT.

The degree of operating leverage may be related to the phases of development of the product life cycle. As shown in Figure 6-3, the degree of operating leverage is high during the expansion phase of the product life cycle. During this phase, profits expand at a more rapid pace than sales. However, profits peak

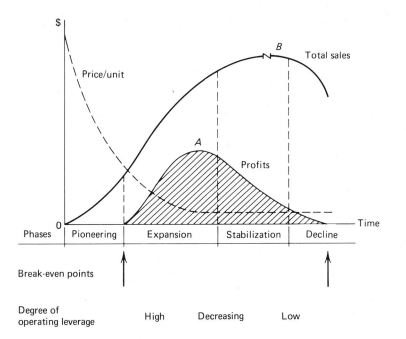

Figure 6-3   The product life cycle and operating leverage.

(point *A*) before sales (point *B*); and the degree of operating leverage decreases throughout the declining phase of the product life cycle until there are losses.

Nonlinear Break-Even Charts

As previously noted, the break-even analysis is based on three assumptions that provide a useful starting point for analyzing revenue/cost relationships. Now the assumptions (about fixed selling price, variable costs being a fixed percentage of sales, and that the level of fixed costs cannot change) are relaxed. Figure 6-4 shows two examples of nonlinear break-even charts. Figure 6-4*a* shows that both revenues and variable costs are nonlinear. Such a pattern can occur when prices are reduced in order to increase sales volume, and variable costs per unit decline over a certain range of sales, and then increase. In this chart, there are two break-even points. The upper break-even point is a result of rising variable costs. The costs of making the sales (commissions, phone, travel, etc.) exceeded the revenue from the sales.

  Figure 6-4*b* shows that the level of fixed costs increases at certain levels of sales. This can occur when a firm must obtain additional warehouse facilities, office space, and delivery trucks to service higher levels of sales. Thus break-even analysis can be modified to take various pricing policies and changing costs into account.

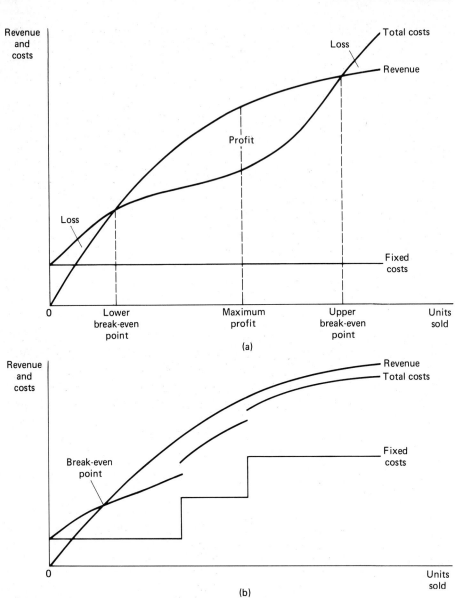

Figure 6-4 Nonlinear break-even charts.

ADDITIONAL USES OF BREAK-EVEN ANALYSIS

In a recent article, Stephen Hawk and Charles Kroncke explained how to use break-even analysis to assist in making decisions involving pricing and the rate of return.[5]

[5] Stephen L. Hawk and Charles O. Kroncke, "The Break Even Concept: A Guide to Profitable Decision Making," *Managerial Planning*, May/June 1977, pp. 11–14, 28.

Table 6-4   Example of Break-Even Analysis for Pricing Decision

Price[†] (1)	Sales forecast (2)	Break-even (3)	Contribution margin[‡] (4)	EBIT at sales forecast (5)
$2.80	30,000	25,000	$1.60	$ 8,000
2.30	50,000	36,363	1.10	15,000
2.00	80,000	50,000	0.80	24,000
1.70	120,000	80,000	0.50	20,000
1.50	140,000	133,333	0.30	2,000

[†]Assumes fixed costs = $40,000, variable cost per unit = $1.20.
[‡]Contribution margin = price − variable costs. Contribution margin less fixed costs = EBIT.
Source: Stephen L. Hawk and Charles O. Kroncke, "The Break Even Concept: A Guide to Profitable Decision Making," *Managerial Planning*, May/June 1977, pp. 11–14, 28.

Pricing Decision

Pricing new products or changing the prices of existing products is an important decision. Table 6-4 shows an example of how break-even analysis can be used in pricing decisions. Assume that the marketing department developed the sales forecasts (column 2) based on the prices shown in column 1. Notice that there is a downward-sloping demand curve for the product, which means that the volume of sales increases when the price is reduced. Further assume that the variable cost is $1.20 per unit and the fixed cost is $40,000. Based on this information, it was possible to determine the EBIT for each sales forecast. As shown in column 5, the largest EBIT is attained when the price is $2 per unit. However, it is premature to select $2 per unit as the final price because additional information concerning the rate of return may be taken into account.

Rate-of-Return Planning

The following example demonstrates how break-even analysis can be used in connection with rate-of-return planning. The data presented in Table 6-5 use

Table 6-5   Example of Break-Even Analysis for Planning Rate of Return

Price (1)	Sales forecast (2)	Contribution margin (3)	Fixed costs (4)	Asset investment (5)	Break-even (6)	EBIT at sales forecast (7)	Rate of return (8)	Operating leverage (9)
$2.80	30,000	$1.60	$40,000	$200,000	$ 25,000	$ 8,000	0.04	6.0
2.30	50,000	1.10	40,000	200,000	36,000	15,000	0.075	3.67
2.00	80,000	0.80	48,000	240,000	60,000	16,000	0.067	4.0
1.70	120,000	0.50	50,000	250,000	100,000	10,000	0.04	6.0
1.50	140,000	0.30	50,000	250,000	166,667	8,000	0.032	5.25

Source: Stephen L. Hawk and Charles O. Kroncke, "The Break Even Concept: A Guide to Profitable Decision Making," *Managerial Planning*, May/June 1977, pp. 11–14, 28.

the same sales forecast and prices that were used in the previous exhibit; but the levels of fixed costs (column 4) and assets (column 5) increase with the volume of sales.

A careful examination of the data presented in Table 6-5 reveals that the $2 price per unit produces the largest profit (column 7). However, this price does not give the best solution in terms of rate of return on investment. At that price and its associated volume, a total investment in assets of $240,000 produces a rate of return of 0.067, or 6.7 percent (column 8). If the sales price were $2.30, the volume of sales would be smaller (50,000 vs. 80,000), but the total invest- ment in assets would be only $200,000, which produces a 7.5 percent rate of return.

The analysis can be expanded to take into account the degree of operating leverage (column 9) that was discussed previously. If the OL is considered a mea- sure of potential changes in profits—or risk, the $2.30 price appears to be the least risky price. In addition, it provides the highest rate of return on assets and does not require an additional investment of $40,000. In this example, the $2.30 price is the best solution because it provides the highest rate of return with the least amount of risk.

CONCLUSION

Break-even analysis is one of several tools that may be used to evaluate partic- ular strategies. Like any analytical tool, it has shortcomings. Therefore, break- even analysis should be used in conjunction with net present value or the in- ternal rate of return, which will be explained in Chapter 8. The strength of break-even analysis is that it is relatively easy to calculate, and it provides im- portant information about break-even sales, revenues, pricing, and other factors. Break-even analysis assumes, as do other analytical techniques, that the data are reliable. If sales and cost estimates are inaccurate, the break-even analysis will give unreliable results. Lockheed estimated incorrectly the total demand for wide-bodied commercial jet aircraft and their costs; and the decision to build the L-1011 TriStar, which was based largely upon break-even analysis, almost resulted in their bankruptcy. The fault, of course, was unreliable data, not break- even analysis. Nevertheless, there are several lessons to be learned from Lock- heed's experience.

1   Do not rely on one analytical technique. Other methods for analyzing the problem should be examined.
2   The output of such techniques is only as good as the input.

All the analytical techniques that are presented here assume that the data are reasonable estimates.

QUESTIONS[†]

1 What are the three underlying assumptions of linear break-even analysis?
2 Assume that

F = $50,000
P = $4
V = $2

What is Q if P is $3?
3 What is the relationship, if any, between operating leverage and financial risk?
4 How is operating leverage related to the life cycle?
5 In Table 6-5, the solution that was presented was a price of $2.30 because it provided the highest rate of return with the least amount of risk. Is this criterion always appropriate?

BIBLIOGRAPHY

Friedland, Seymour. *Principles of Financial Management*. Cambridge, Mass.: Winthrop Publishers, Inc., 1978.

Gitman, Lawrence J. *Principles of Managerial Finance*, 2d ed. New York: Harper & Row, Publishers, Incorporated, 1979.

Tucker, S. *The Break-Even System: A Tool for Profit Planning*. Englewood Cliffs, N.J.: Prentice-Hall, Inc., 1963.

Woelfel, Charles J. *Guides for Profit Planning*. Washington, D.C.: Small Business Administration, 1975.

[†]Selected solutions at end of book.

Chapter 7

How to Use Compound
Interest

Several techniques may be used to determine the economic viability of particular projects or strategies. As noted in the previous chapter, Lockheed Aircraft Corporation used break-even analysis to evaluate their strategy of entering the market for wide-bodied jets with the L-1011 TriStar. The next chapter deals with other techniques that may be used to make similar decisions. Those techniques that discount cash flows (net present value and the internal rate of return) are based on variants of compound-interest equations. Accordingly, this chapter has two objectives. The first objective is to provide the background that is necessary to deal with discounting cash flows. The second objective is to explain how compound interest may be used to solve some typical business problems. For example, the Mitchusson Jewelry Company is in the expansion phase of its life cycle, and the assets of that company are increasing at the rate of 18 percent per year. How many years will it take until the assets of the firm double? Such information is important because the existing facilities are not large enough to handle the increased sales that will generate twice the volume of assets; so the company will have to move to a new location. Equally important, financing twice the volume of assets will require additional equity, which means that the company will have either to take on additional partners or to incorporate and sell stock to the public. Thus the company can use compound interest to provide information about the timing of decisions to move to a new location and obtain additional equity capital.

Another typical business problem concerns Joanne Beauty Consultants. This company is going to bid on a contract to provide management services for a chain of beauty salons. The contract will begin 3 years from now, and the beauty salons will pay $100,000 per year for 15 years. Joanne Beauty Consultants wants to earn 10 percent annually. How much should the company bid for the contract? The solutions to the problems of the Mitchusson Jewelry Company and Joanne Beauty Consultants are explained in this chapter.

COMPOUND INTEREST

A thorough understanding of compound interest is necessary before one can understand present value, annuities, and discounting cash flows. Compound interest is a relatively easy concept to understand. Compound interest means that interest is paid on the principal and interest earned in the previous period of time. It works in the following manner. Assume that $100 is deposited in a bank at the beginning of the year 1. The $100 is the *principal* amount at the beginning of the year. If the principal amount is left on deposit for the entire year, the bank will pay 6 percent interest at the end of that year. Therefore, the future value at the end of 1 year is the principal amount plus the interest earned during the year of $106 [see Equation (7-1)].

$$\text{Future value at the end of year 1} = \$100\,(1 + 0.06) = \$106 \qquad (7\text{-}1)$$

The future value at the end of year 1 becomes the principal amount at the beginning of year 2. If the new principal amount remains on deposit for the entire year, the bank will pay interest on that amount at the end of the second year. As shown in Equation (7-2), the future value at the end of the second year is $112.36.

$$\text{Future value at the end of year 2} = \$106\,(1 + 0.06) = \$112.36 \qquad (7\text{-}2)$$

The important point is that interest is computed at the end of each period, and it is added to the principal at the beginning of that period. The total amount (principal and interest from period 1) is considered the principal at the beginning of the second period. At the end of the second period, interest is computed again. Therefore, interest is paid on interest, and this is how the term "compound interest" originated.

The same process can be explained in terms of equations. The compound-interest equation that is developed here is the basis of all the equations that will be developed throughout the remainder of the chapter. Therefore, understanding the basic compound-interest equation is very important. The basic compound-interest equation can be developed as follows using this notation.

FV = future value, or the value at the end of some period
PV = present value, or the principal that was the beginning amount
I = dollar amount of interest earned per period expressed as $
i = interest rate per period expressed as a decimal
n = number of periods
m = number of intrayear periods
ln = natural logarithm

The future value of a sum of money to be received at the end of one year FV_1 may be determined by

$$\begin{aligned} FV_1 &= PV_0 + I \\ &= PV_0 + PV_0\,(i) \\ &= PV_0\,(1 + i) \end{aligned} \tag{7-3}$$

Equation (7-3) shows that the future value at the end of year 1 is equal to the beginning amount PV_0 times the interest factor $(1 + i)$. For example, where $PV_0 = \$100$ and the interest rate is 6 percent, FV_1 is

$$FV_1 = \$100\,(1 + 0.06) = \$106$$

If the $100 were left on deposit for 2 years, the future value at the end of the second year could be determined by

$$\begin{aligned} FV_2 &= PV_0\,(1 + i)\,(1 + i) = PV_0\,(1 + 1)^2 \\ FV_2 &= \$100\,(1 + 0.06)\,(1 + 0.06) = \$100\,(1 + 0.06)^2 = \$100\,(1.1236) \\ &= \$112.36 \end{aligned}$$

Similarly, if the $100 were left on deposit for 3 years, the future value at the end of that period could be computed by

$$\begin{aligned} FV_3 &= PV_0\,(1 + i)\,(1 + i)\,(1 + i) = PV_0\,(1 + i)^3 \\ FV_3 &= \$100\,(1 + 0.06)^3 = \$100\,(1.1910) \\ &= \$119.10 \end{aligned}$$

Thus the future value at the end of any year n can be determined by the general equation for compound interest [Equation (7-4)].

General Equation for Compound Interest

$$FV_n = PV_0\,(1 + i)^n \tag{7-4}$$

Using Compound Interest

The general equation for compound interest is used in the following manner. First, if $100 is left on deposit for 25 years and the bank pays 6 percent interest annually, the future value at the end of that period is

$$FV_{25} = PV_0 (1 + i)^{25} = \$100 (1 + 0.06)^{25} = \$100 (4.292) = \$429.20$$

The interest factor used in the equation can be computed, or one can use a compound-interest table like the one shown in Table 7-1. The interest factor (4.292) is found by reading down the 6 percent column until the row marked 25 years.

Second, suppose that a firm has assets of $63 million and it is growing at a rate of 8 percent per year. The asset size of the firm at the end of say 5 years can be determined by multiplying the present value of $63 million by the interest factor 1.469 that is found in Table 7-1 by reading down the 8 percent column until the row marked 5 years.

$$FV_5 = PV_0 (1 + i)^5 = \$63 (1.469) = \$92.57 \text{ million}$$

Third, compound interest also can be used to determine the approximate length of time required to double the present value. When the interest factor shown in Table 7-1 is 2.0, the approximate number of years required to double the present value can be read off the years column at the left-hand side of the table. For example, read down the 5 percent column until the interest factor reads 2.079. This figure is in the 15-year row. Thus a firm with assets of $12 million that is growing at 5 percent per year will double in size in about 15 years. The time required for the present value to double also may be calculated by the rule of 72, which will be discussed shortly.

The interest factor $(1 + i)^n$ can be computed from a hand-held calculator, or you may use a compound-interest table. The advantage of the hand-held calculator is that it can be used for unlimited combinations of time periods and interest rates, whereas compound interest tables are limited to a relatively few time periods and selected interest rates. For example, you would have to interpolate if the interest rate were 8.75 percent and the time period was 3.5 years. Another advantage of the hand-held calculator is greater accuracy. Many hand-held calculators provide more significant digits than are shown in most tables. In spite of the physical limitations of tables, they are very useful when you do not have a calculator.

The Power of Compound Interest

Compound interest is a powerful force. It is particularly powerful when high interest rates are involved for long periods of time. Consider the growth of $1000 that is compounded at 6 and 10 percent for various periods of time (see

Table 7-1 Compound Sums of $1 Received at End of Period

Year	1%	2%	3%	4%	5%	6%	7%	8%	9%	10%	15%	20%
1	1.010	1.020	1.030	1.040	1.050	1.060	1.070	1.080	1.090	1.100	1.150	1.200
2	1.020	1.040	1.061	1.082	1.102	1.124	1.145	1.166	1.188	1.210	1.322	1.440
3	1.030	1.061	1.093	1.125	1.158	1.191	1.225	1.260	1.295	1.331	1.521	1.728
4	1.041	1.082	1.126	1.170	1.216	1.262	1.311	1.360	1.412	1.464	1.749	2.074
5	1.051	1.104	1.159	1.217	1.276	1.338	1.403	1.469	1.539	1.611	2.011	2.488
6	1.062	1.126	1.194	1.265	1.340	1.419	1.501	1.587	1.677	1.772	2.313	2.986
7	1.072	1.149	1.230	1.316	1.407	1.504	1.606	1.714	1.828	1.949	2.660	3.583
8	1.083	1.172	1.267	1.369	1.477	1.594	1.718	1.851	1.993	2.144	3.059	4.300
9	1.094	1.195	1.305	1.423	1.551	1.689	1.838	1.999	2.172	2.358	3.518	5.160
10	1.105	1.219	1.344	1.480	1.629	1.791	1.967	2.159	2.367	2.594	4.046	6.192
11	1.116	1.243	1.384	1.539	1.710	1.808	2.105	2.332	2.580	2.853	4.652	7.430
12	1.127	1.268	1.426	1.601	1.796	2.012	2.252	2.518	2.813	3.138	5.350	8.916
13	1.138	1.294	1.469	1.665	1.886	2.133	2.410	2.720	3.066	3.452	6.153	10.699
14	1.149	1.319	1.513	1.732	1.980	2.261	2.579	2.937	3.342	3.797	7.076	12.839
15	1.161	1.346	1.558	1.801	2.079	2.397	2.759	3.172	3.642	4.177	8.137	15.407
16	1.173	1.373	1.605	1.873	2.183	2.540	2.952	3.426	3.970	4.595	9.358	18.488
17	1.184	1.400	1.653	1.948	2.292	2.693	3.159	3.700	4.328	5.054	10.761	22.186
18	1.196	1.428	1.702	2.026	2.407	2.854	3.380	3.996	4.717	5.560	12.375	26.623
19	1.208	1.457	1.754	2.107	2.527	3.026	3.617	4.316	5.142	6.116	14.232	31.948
20	1.220	1.486	1.806	2.191	2.653	3.207	3.870	4.661	5.604	6.728	16.367	38.338
25	1.282	1.641	2.094	2.666	3.386	4.292	5.427	6.848	8.623	10.835	32.919	95.396
30	1.348	1.811	2.427	3.243	4.322	5.743	7.612	10.063	13.268	17.449	66.212	237.376

Table 7-2 The Growth of $1000 Compounded at 6 and 10 Percent Annually

	6%	10%	End of year	Percentage difference between future values
$1000 will grow to	$ 1,338	$ 1,611	5	20
	1,791	2,594	10	45
	3,207	6,727	20	81
	18,420	117,390	50	537
	339,302	13,780,612	100	3961

Table 7-2). The future value of $1000 compounded at 10 percent is significantly higher than the future value compounded at 6 percent. Observe how the difference between the two columns increases as length of time increases. At the end of 5 years, the future value of the amounts compounded at 10 percent is 20 percent higher than the amounts compounded at 6 percent. At the end of 100 years, the future value of the amounts compounded at 10 percent was 3961 percent higher than that of the amounts compounded at 6 percent!

The Rule of 72

The power of compound interest can be demonstrated by the length of time necessary for the principal amounts to double in value when compounded at different rates of interest. The approximate length of time can be determined by dividing the interest rate into 72. For example, if the principal amount is compounded at 2 percent, it will double in about 36 years. If it is compounded at 6 percent, the principal amount will double in 12 years. The time is reduced to 7.2 years when the interest rate is 10 percent and 4.8 years when the interest rate is 15 percent.

The power of compounding has some very important implications for strategic planning. The assets of the Mitchusson Jewelry Company are growing at 18 percent per year and will double in 4 years! In the next 10 years, the assets of that firm will grow to more than 10 times their original amount! Many firms are not prepared to cope with such growth.

The Reinvestment Rate

The previous section demonstrated that compound interest is a powerful force. The "power" stems from the fact that all the funds are reinvested at some given rate of interest. When this so-called "reinvestment rate" assumption does not occur, the "power" of compound interest is reduced drastically. In order to illustrate the difference between the total returns when funds are reinvested or withdrawn, consider $1000 compounded annually at 9 percent for 5 years. As shown in the top panel of Table 7-3, all the funds are reinvested at 9 percent. The future value at the end of the fifth year is $1538.62, and the total interest

Table 7-3 $1000 Compounded Annually at 9 Percent

	All funds reinvested at 9%	
Year-end		
0	PV = $1000.00	I = $ 0.00
1	FV = 1090.00	90.00
2	FV = 1188.10	98.10
3	FV = 1295.02	106.92
4	FV = 1411.58	116.56
5	FV = 1538.62	127.04
	Total	I = $538.62
	Interest payments withdrawn	
0	PV = 1000	I = 0.00
1	FV = 1000	90.00
2	FV = 1000	90.00
3	FV = 1000	90.00
4	FV = 1000	90.00
5	FV = 1000	90.00
	Total	I = $450.00

earned amounts to $538.62. The data presented in the lower panel of Table 7-3 show what will happen if all the interest payments were withdrawn at the end of every period. The future value is $1000 and the total interest payments amount to $450. Note that the interest rate in both examples shown in Table 7-3 is 9 percent. Nevertheless, the final amounts differ significantly because all the funds were reinvested and compounded at 9 percent in the first case and none were reinvested or compounded in the second case.

Now let's look at the same problem from a slightly different point of view. Assume that an investor buys a 10 percent coupon bond for $1000 and the bond will mature in 15 years. For simplicity, assume that the coupon payments are made at the end of each year. As shown in Table 7-4, if all the money received

Table 7-4   Selected Returns from a 10 Percent Coupon Bond with 15 Years to Maturity

Reinvestment rate, % (1)	Total income from coupons and interest earned (2)	Annual realized rate of return, % (3)
0	$1500	6.3
6	2328	8.3
8	2715	9.1
10	3177	10.0
12	3728	10.9
14	4384	11.9

from coupon payments is withdrawn, the total income over the life of the bond will be $1500 and the annual realized rate of return will be 6.3 percent. If all the funds are reinvested, the annual realized rate of return takes the total income into account.[1] However, at say 6 percent, the total income will increase, but the annual realized rate of return will amount to only 8.3 percent. Only when all the funds are reinvested at 10 percent does the investor realize a 10 percent rate of return. If the funds can be reinvested at higher interest rates, the annual realized rate of return will exceed 10 percent.

The point of both examples is that the reinvestment-rate assumption applies any time compound interest or one of its variants is used.

Compounding for Periods of Less than 1 Year

Sometimes it is necessary to compound interest more than once a year. For example, interest on bank loans may be computed on a quarterly or monthly basis. Interest on some types of business loans is computed on a daily basis. Recall that the general equation for computing compound interest is

$$FV_n = PV_0 (1 + i)^n \tag{7-4}$$

For other periods of time, divide the interest rate by the number of intrayear periods m, and multiply the exponent n by the same number. Thus the equation

---

[1] In the case of a bond, the cash flow or coupon income is the same each year. Consequently, the total income is equivalent to the amount of an ordinary annuity (S_n). After n periods, the total addition to income is

$$S_n = R \, \frac{(1 + i)^n - 1}{i}$$

where R = periodic payments
i = reinvestment rate
n = number of periods
S_n = column 2 in Table 7-4

The annual compound return that investors receive from their original investment over the holding period is called the annual realized return a, which may be determined by

$$\frac{S_n + P}{P} = (1 + a)^n$$

where S_n = amount of an ordinary annuity
P = par value of the bond ($1000)
a = interest rate per period
n = number of periods

For additional information, see Benton Gup, "The Impact of Reinvestment Rates on the Realized Rate of Return," *California Management Review*, winter 1974, pp. 91–92.

**Table 7-5 Effects of Compounding 6 Percent
for Periods of Less than 1 Year[†]**

Compounding period	Times per year m	Annual yield, %
Annual	1	6.000
Semiannual	2	6.091
Quarterly	4	6.136
Monthly	12	6.168
Weekly	52	6.180
Daily	365	6.183
Continuous	∞	6.183

[†]Based on the equation $FV_n = PV_0 \left(1 + \dfrac{i}{m}\right)^{nm}$

for periods of less than 1 year is

$$FV_n = PV_0 \left(1 + \frac{i}{m}\right)^{nm} \tag{7-5}$$

The symbol m is the number of intrayear periods or the number of times that interest is paid per year. When interest is paid annually, there is only one period and m is equal to 1. When $m = 1$, Equations (7-4) and (7-5) are identical. If interest is paid quarterly, there are four intrayear periods and m is equal to 4. Accordingly, Equation (7-5) becomes

$$FV_n = PV_0 \left(1 + \frac{i}{4}\right)^{n4}$$

Similarly, if interest were paid monthly or weekly, the number of intrayear periods would be 12 or 52, respectively.

The number of times that interest is paid per year is directly related to the annual yield. Table 7-5 shows the effects of compounding 6 percent for various periods of 1 year or less. When 6 percent is paid only once a year, the annual yield is 6 percent. If interest were compounded on a monthly basis, the annual yield would be 6.168 percent. The annual yield increases as the number of compounding periods increases. However, the maximum annual yield is obtained when compounding is continuous. In this example, the maximum yield is 6.183 percent.[2]

The number of compounding periods has its greatest effect when one is dealing with high interest rates over a long period of time. Table 7-6 shows the growth of $1000 at 6 and 10 percent compounded annually and quarterly for various periods of time. At the end of the first 5 years, the difference between

[2]The continuous yield was calculated by $e^i = (2.718)^{0.06}$.

Table 7-6 The Growth of $1000 at 6 and 10% Compounded Annually and Quarterly

6% compounded		10% compounded		Years
				At the
Annually	Quarterly	Annually	Quarterly	end of
$ 1,338	$ 1,347	$ 1,611	$ 1,663	5
18,420	19,643	117,390	139,563	50
339,302	385,489	13,780,612	19,478,080	100

the amounts compounded annually and quarterly is relatively small. The difference is $9 at 6 percent and $52 at 10 percent. However, the difference between the amounts compounded annually and quarterly increased dramatically as the length of time increased. Moreover, as previously noted, the difference was greater when the principal was compounded at 10 percent than when it was compounded at 6 percent. At the end of 100 years, there was a $46,187 difference between the future values of the amounts compounded annually and quarterly at 6 percent, and a $5,697,468 percent difference between the future values of the amounts compounded at 10 percent. Firms borrowing, lending, or investing over long periods of time when interest rates are high should be aware of the effects of compounding interest more than once a year.

How Long Will It Take?

Superfine Manufacturing Company has $10 million in assets and is growing at a rate of 10 percent per year. The chairman of the board, a firm believer in planning, wants to know how long it will take until the company reaches $15 million in assets. The answer to this question can be found by using the compound-interest table (Table 7-1) or a modification of the general compound-interest equation. In order to use the compound-interest table to solve the problem, divide the future value by the present value to obtain the interest factor:

$$(1 + i)^n = \frac{FV}{PV} = \frac{\$15 \text{ million}}{\$10 \text{ million}} = 1.500$$

Since the company is growing at 10 percent per year, the interest rate i is 10 percent $(1 + 0.10)$.

$$(1 + 0.1)^n = 1.500$$

Now that both the interest rate (0.10 percent) and the interest factor (1.500) are known, the number of years n can be determined from the table. In fact, any time that two of the three parts of the table (years, interest factor, and interest rate) are known, one can determine the third. For example, read down the 10 percent column to find the interest factor that is close to 1.500.

Year	Percent 1% ... 5% ... 8% ... 10%
1	1.100
2	1.210
3	1.331
4	1.464
5	1.611

The interest factor is between 1.464 and 1.611. These two interest factors are the factors for years 4 and 5. Interpolating the difference between the interest factors gives the answer to the problem as 4.2 years.

Interpolation

$$\begin{array}{ll} & \text{Year } 5 = 1.611 \\ \text{Less} & \text{Year } 4 = \underline{1.464} \\ & \phantom{\text{Year } 4 = }0.147 \\ & \text{Year ? } = 1.500 \\ & \text{Year } 4 = \underline{1.464} \\ & \phantom{\text{Year } 4 = }0.036 \end{array}$$

$$0.036/0.147 = 0.24 \text{ years}$$
$$n = \text{year } 4 + 0.2 = 4.2 \text{ years}$$

The alternate method for solving the problem is to use Equation (7-6). Because the equation uses natural logarithms, one must have a table of natural logarithms ln or use a hand calculator that has natural log capability.

$$\begin{aligned} \text{Number of periods } n &= \frac{\ln (FV/PV)}{\ln (1 + i)} \\ &= \frac{\ln (1.5)}{\ln (1.1)} \\ &= \frac{0.4055}{0.0953} = 4.25 \\ &= 4.2 \text{ years} \end{aligned} \qquad (7\text{-}6)$$

What Is the Rate of Growth?

Leroy Cross is the sales manager for Southwest Distributors. He sold 5200 truck tires and has a target of 8300 tires 3 years from now. What rate of growth will Leroy have to attain in order to reach his goal? Once again, the answer can be determined by using the compound-interest table or an equation. In this problem, the number of years ($n = 3$) and the interest factor (FV/PV = 8300/5200 = 1.596) are available. The equation for determining the interest per period is

$$
\begin{aligned}
\text{Interest per period } i &= (\text{FV/PV})^{1/n} - 1 \\
&= (1.596)^{1/3} - 1 \\
&= (1.596)^{0.333} - 1 \\
&= 1.1686 - 1 \\
&= 16.86 \text{ percent}
\end{aligned}
\tag{7-7}
$$

And the answer is that sales will have to grow at 16.86 percent per year to reach 8300 at the end of 3 years.

PRESENT VALUE

How Much Is It Worth Today?

Present value (PV) is one of the most important formulations of the compound-interest equation. Present value indicates how much dollars that will be received in the future are worth today. Knowing how much future cash flows are worth today is important because a time value is associated with money. The time value of money means that having money today is worth more than having the promise of the same amount 1 year from now. Receiving $100 today is better than receiving $100 one year from now. The general idea is that a bird in the hand is worth two in the bush. Moreover, present value is the basis for all the discounted cash flow techniques, such as net present value, that are used in capital budgeting and other types of decisions. Such techniques are explained in the next chapter. The term "discounted cash flow" means determining the present value of cash flows. Equally important, the terms "discount rate," "capitalization rate," and "interest rate" are used interchangeably, and they refer to i in the equations.

$$
\text{Present value PV} = \text{FV} \cdot \frac{1}{(1+i)^n}
\tag{7-8}
$$

The following example illustrates how to use Equation (7-8) to determine present value. Eric Carol has been promised a $10,000 bonus at the end of 3 years if he finishes the construction project on time. If Eric expects to earn a 10 percent return on his investments, how much is the bonus worth today? The answer is

$$
\text{PV} = \text{FV} \cdot \frac{1}{(1+i)^n}
$$

$$= \$10,000 \cdot \frac{1}{(1 + 0.10)^3}$$

$$= \$10,000 \cdot \frac{1}{1.331}$$

$$= \$10,000 \,(0.7513)$$

$$= \$7513.00$$

An alternate method of obtaining the interest factor used for solving present-value problems is to use a present-value table such as the one shown in Table 7-7. The present-value table is used in the same way one uses the compound-interest table that was discussed previously. The interest factor $(1 + i)^n$ is found in the 10 percent column and the row for the third year (0.751). Another example will clarify the use of the table.

Laddie Dog Foods expects sales of $21 million for the next 2 years and sales of $25 million in the following 3 years. If they discount the expected sales at 14 percent, how much are the future sales worth today? The answer can be found by summing the products of the future value times the interest factors for each of the years. The interest factors are from the 14 percent column for each year. The answer is that the present value of the $117 million in future sales is $79,216 when discounted at 14 percent interest.

Table 7-7 Present Value of $1 Received at the End of Period[†]

Years	6%	8%	10%	12%	14%	16%	20%
1	0.943	0.926	0.909	0.893	0.877	0.862	0.833
2	0.890	0.857	0.826	0.797	0.769	0.743	0.694
3	0.840	0.794	0.751	0.712	0.675	0.641	0.579
4	0.792	0.735	0.683	0.635	0.592	0.552	0.482
5	0.747	0.681	0.621	0.567	0.519	0.476	0.402
6	0.705	0.630	0.564	0.507	0.456	0.410	0.335
7	0.665	0.583	0.513	0.452	0.400	0.354	0.279
8	0.627	0.540	0.467	0.404	0.351	0.305	0.233
9	0.592	0.500	0.424	0.361	0.308	0.263	0.194
10	0.558	0.463	0.386	0.322	0.270	0.227	0.162
11	0.527	0.429	0.350	0.287	0.237	0.195	0.135
12	0.497	0.397	0.319	0.257	0.208	0.168	0.112
13	0.469	0.368	0.290	0.229	0.182	0.145	0.093
14	0.442	0.340	0.263	0.205	0.160	0.125	0.078
15	0.417	0.315	0.239	0.183	0.140	0.108	0.065

[†]Tables 7-1 and 7-7 are reciprocals. Thus the reciprocal of $1 compounded at 6 percent for 5 years is $1/(1.06)5 = 1/(1.338) = 0.747$, which is the present value of $1 at 6 percent for 5 years. Similarly, the reciprocal of 0.747 is 1.338, which is the compound amount of 6 percent for 5 years.

Year-end	Future value	X	Interest factor	=	Total
1	$21 million		0.877		$18,417 million
2	$21 million		0.769		$16,149 million
3	$25 million		0.675		$16,875 million
4	$25 million		0.592		$14,800 million
5	$25 million		0.519		$12,975 million
Future value = $117 million			Present value	=	$79,216 million

ANNUITIES

The final formulation of the general compound-interest equation that is discussed is for an annuity. An annuity is defined as a series of periodic payments that are usually made in equal amounts for a specified period of time. For example, lease payments are an annuity. The cash flow from some capital investment projects may be considered annuities. The reason for discussing annuities here is that knowing how to compute the present value of an annuity can save time in determining the present value of a future stream of income.

Types of Annuities

There are many different types of annuities. Some annuities begin and end on definite dates. Others begin on a definite date but the length of the term of the annuity is indefinite. In some cases, payments are made at the end of each period of time, and in others they are made at the beginning of the period. Moreover, the payment date may or may not coincide with the dates that interest is computed. In order to avoid confusion, the examples used in this chapter assume that payments and interest are made at the end of each period of time and that the term of the annuity is specified. Because of these assumptions, the equations presented here may not be applicable for some other types of annuities.

Present Value of an Annuity

The present value of an annuity, like the present value that was discussed previously, can be determined by using a table (Table 7-8) or an equation [Equation (7-9)].

Before working an example, take a close look at Table 7-8, which shows the present value of an annuity. The interest factors that are presented in Table 7-8 can be derived from the interest factors from the present-value table (Table 7-7). For example, the interest factor for the present value of 6 percent for 1 year in both tables is 0.943. The interest factor for the present value of 6 percent for 2 years in Table 7-7 is 0.890. When these two interest factors are added together, the sum is 1.833 (0.943 + 0.890 = 1.833). This is the same interest factor that appears in Table 7-8 as the present value of an annuity at 6 percent for 2 years. Similarly, one could add the interest factors for 3 years from Table 7-8 and

Table 7-8   Present Value of an Annuity ($1)

Years	6%	8%	10%	12%	14%	16%	20%
1	0.943	0.926	0.909	0.893	0.877	0.862	0.833
2	1.833	1.783	1.736	1.690	1.647	1.605	1.528
3	2.673	2.577	2.487	2.402	2.322	2.246	2.106
4	3.465	3.312	3.170	3.037	2.914	2.798	2.589
5	4.212	3.993	3.791	3.605	3.433	3.274	2.991
6	4.917	4.623	4.355	4.111	3.889	3.685	3.326
7	5.582	5.206	4.868	4.564	4.288	4.039	3.605
8	6.210	5.747	5.335	4.968	4.639	4.344	3.837
9	6.802	6.247	5.759	5.328	4.946	4.607	4.031
10	7.360	6.710	6.145	5.650	5.216	4.833	4.192
11	7.877	7.139	6.495	5.988	5.453	5.029	4.327
12	8.384	7.536	6.814	6.194	5.660	5.197	4.439
13	8.853	7.904	7.103	6.424	5.842	5.342	4.533
14	9.295	8.244	7.367	6.628	6.002	5.468	4.611
15	9.712	8.559	7.606	6.811	6.142	5.575	4.675

arrive at the same interest factor that is shown for 3 years in Table 7-8. Thus, as noted earlier, computing the value of an annuity is a timesaving device. It is easier to find one number in an annuity table than it is to find six or seven numbers from the present-value table. Consider the following problem.

The Bloch Realty Company is going to receive $1000 a year for the next 4 years. The payments are made at the end of each year, and the discount rate is 6 percent. How much is that future stream of income worth today? The solution to the problem is shown in Table 7-9. As shown in the bottom panel of Table 7-9, the $1000 payment is multiplied by the interest factor that is taken from Table 7-8, and the answer is $3465. The top panel shows how the payment from each period is discounted and then summed to arrive at the present value. The middle panel shows the computations for each period. The interest factors used in that computation can be found in Table 7-7, the present-value table. However, when all those interest factors are summed, they total 3.465, which is the interest factor that is found in Table 7-8, the annuity table.

Two problems were presented at the beginning of this chapter. The first problem was solved on page 108. The second problem can be solved by determining the present value of an annuity. Joanne Beauty Consultants is going to bid on a contract to provide management services for a chain of beauty salons. The contract will begin 3 years from now, and the beauty salons will pay $100,000 per year for 15 years. Joanne Beauty Consultants wants to earn 10 percent annually. How much should they bid for the contract? The first step is to determine the present value of $100,000 three years from now ($75,100). The interest factor (0.751) was taken from the present-value table (Table 7-7) because the first payment will not be made until the end of the third year. Next, the interest factor for the 15-year annuity at 10 percent (7.606), which comes from Table 7-8, was multiplied by $75,100 to arrive at $571,210.60.

Table 7-9   Present Value of a $1000 Annuity at 6 Percent for 4 Years

	Now		Years		
Present value of receipts	0	1	2	3	4

$PMT_1(1+i) \leftarrow PMT_1$ PMT_2 PMT_3 PMT_4

$PMT_2(1+i)^2 \leftarrow$

$PMT_3(1+i)^3 \leftarrow$

$PMT_4(1+i)^4 \leftarrow$

Sum = present value

	0	1	2	3	4
	$943 $\leftarrow$	$1000 (0.943)	$1000 (0.890)	$1000 (0.840)	$1000 (0.792)
	890 $\leftarrow$				
	840 $\leftarrow$				
	792 $\leftarrow$				
Present value =	$3465				

Present value = PMT (interest factor)
         = $1000 (3.465)
         = $3465
    PMT = payment for period

1 Present value of $100,000 three years from now at 10 percent
         $100,000 (interest factor from Table 7-7)
         $100,000 (0.751)
      = $75,100

2 Present value of 15-year annuity at 10 percent
         Interest factor = 7.606 (from Table 7-8)

3 Present value of $100,000 three years from now multiplied by the interest factor for the annuity equals
         $75,100
      X   7.606
      = $571,210.06

An alternate method that gives a slightly different answer because of the rounding of values is shown below.

1 Present value of an annuity for 18 years at 10 percent
$$\text{Interest factor} = 8.201$$

2 Less: present value of an annuity for 15 years
$$\text{Interest factor} = \frac{2.487}{5.714}$$

3 Multiplied by $100,000
$$\frac{\times\ \$100,000}{=\ \$571,400}$$

The present value of an annuity can be determined by solving Equation (7-9). For example, assume that an annuity pays $30,000 per year for 10 years and the discount rate is 15 percent. The present value of that annuity is $150,160.00. As previously noted, the equations can be solved on hand-held calculators, thus giving the user considerably more flexibility than using tables to determine interest factors.

Present Value of an Annuity PV_a

$$PV_a = PMT\ \frac{1 - (1 + i)^{-n}}{i} \tag{7-9}$$

where PMT = payment per period

$$PV_a = \$30,000\ \frac{1 - (1 + 0.15)^{-10}}{0.15}$$

$$= \$30,000\ \frac{1 - (0.2472)}{0.15}$$

$$= \$150,160.00$$

Listing of Equations

Table 7-10 provides a convenient listing of all the equations that were discussed in the chapter and some that were not discussed. The only equation that was discussed in connection with annuities was for determining the present value of

Table 7-10 Compound Interest and Other Equations

Compound amounts:

1. Future value
2. Present value

$$FV_n = PV_0(1 + i)^n$$
$$PV_0 = FV_n(1 + i)^{-n}$$

3. Number of periods

$$n = \frac{\ln (FV/PV)}{\ln (1 + i)}$$

4. Interest per period

$$i = \left(\frac{FV}{PV}\right)^{1/n} - 1$$

Annuities:

1. Future value

$$FV_a = PMT \frac{(1 + i)^n - 1}{i}$$

2. Present value

$$PV_a = PMT \frac{1 - (1 + i)^{-n}}{i}$$

3. Payment per period for PV

$$PMT_a = PV_a \frac{i}{1 - (1 + i)^{-n}}$$

4. Payment per period for FV

$$PMT_a = FV_a \frac{i}{(1 + i)^n - 1}$$

5. Number of periods for PV

$$n_a = \frac{\ln [1 - PV (i/PMT)]}{\ln (1 + i)}$$

6. Number of periods for FV

$$n_a = \frac{\ln [1 + FV (i/PMT)]}{\ln (1 + i)}$$

where FV = future value
PV = present value
n = number of periods
i = interest payment per period expressed as a decimal
PMT = payment per period n
ln = natural logarithm
a = annuity

an annuity. The equations for determining the future value of an annuity FV_a and number of periods n_a differ mechanically but not conceptually from their counterparts FV and n, which were discussed under compound interest. Thus it is assumed that the reader will recognize the similarity of the concepts and be able to use the appropriate numbers in the correct equations.

CONCLUSION

The term compound interest refers to interest paid on interest. The concept of compound interest is important because it forms the basis for discounting cash flows, which is explained in the next chapter. Equally important, compound interest is a valuable technique for solving business problems involving rates of growth, the length of time required to reach a particular size, and so on. The equations for compound interest are used to derive the equations for present value and annuities. Present value indicates how much dollars received in the future are worth today. An annuity is a series of periodic payments that are usually made in equal amounts for a specified period of time. Present value and annuities are used extensively in discounting cash flows which is presented next.

QUESTIONS[†]

1 What is the value of $1000 compounded at 10 percent per year for (*a*) 5 years, (*b*) 10 years, (*c*) 20 years, and (*d*) 30 years?
2 What is the value of $1000 compounded at 20 percent per year for (*a*) 5 years, (*b*) 10 years, (*c*) 20 years, and (*d*) 30 years?
3 Explain why the differences between the answers for questions 1 and 2 are so large.
4 What is the value of $1000 to be received 2 years from now if the discount rates are (*a*) 8 percent and (*b*) 16 percent?
5 Five years ago, total sales were $3.5 million and today they are $9.2 million. What was the compound growth rate of sales?

BIBLIOGRAPHY

Gitman, Lawrence J. *Principles of Managerial Finance*, 2d ed. New York: Harper & Row, Publishers, Incorporated, 1979.
Mayer, Raymond R. *Financial Analysis of Investment Alternatives*. Boston, Mass.: Allyn and Bacon, Inc., 1966.
Shao, Stephen P. *Mathematics for Management and Finance*, 2d ed. Cincinnati, Ohio: South-Western Publishing Company, Incorporated, 1969.

[†]Selected solutions at end of book.

Chapter 8

Chapter 8

Investment Decisions

This chapter applies the tools that were developed in the previous chapter. It is divided into two parts. The first part illustrates how present-value concepts are used to determine the value of common stock or the value of any company. An important part of the strategic plans of many companies concerns acquisitions and divestitures. Therefore, they should know the worth of companies that are being bought or sold. The second part of the chapter deals with ranking investment proposals or certain types of corporate strategies such as Lockheed's L-1011 TriStar. In that section, four capital budgeting techniques are discussed.

THE VALUE OF COMMON STOCK

In November 1978, stock prices were low. The Dow Jones Industrial Average declined from 900 in October to a low of 780. Many investors were discouraged by the falling stock prices and wanted to get out of the stock market. Other investors saw this as a golden opportunity to acquire stocks and companies at reasonable values. The real question is how much is the stock of a company worth? This section deals with one method that can be used to determine the "worth" or *intrinsic* value of common stock. The term intrinsic value is the theoretical value of a stock. It is important to keep in mind that the intrinsic value and the current market price are not necessarily the same price. A stock is said to be *undervalued* when the intrinsic value is *more* than the current market value, in other words, when a stock worth $40 per share is selling at $25 per share. Conversely, a stock is *overvalued* when the intrinsic value is *less* than the current market value of the stock. If a stock is worth $40 per share and is selling for $50 per share, it is overvalued.

Dividend-Valuation Method

Dividends are one of the principal determinants of the intrinsic value of common stock. The reasoning behind this statement is explained in the following verse that a farmer told his son.

> A cow for her milk,
> A hen for her eggs,
> And a stock, by heck,
> For her dividends.
>
> An orchard for fruit,
> Bees for their honey,
> And stock, besides,
> For their dividends.[1]

The point is that one does not buy a cow for her cud or a bee for its buzz. They are bought for what one can get out of them—milk and honey. Similarly, investors get dividends from stocks until they are sold.

The intrinsic value of most common stocks can be determined by discounting all the future cash dividends that the company will pay. In other words, the value of a share of common stock is as shown in Equation (8-1). P_0 is the intrinsic value of each share of common stock at current time period 0, which is now; D_1, D_2, and D_t are the cash dividends per share in time periods 1, 2, and t; and k is the discount rate determined by investors. Sometimes k is called the capitalization rate. Whatever k is called, it is the interest rate that is used to determine the present value of future cash dividends. The intrinsic value emerges only if the proper discount rate is used. The determination of this rate will be explained shortly. Sigma (Σ) means summation and ∞ stands for infinity.

$$P_0 = \frac{D_1}{(1 + k)^1} + \frac{D_2}{(1 + k)^2} + \cdots + \frac{D_\infty}{(1 + k)^\infty}$$

$$P_0 = \sum_{t=1}^{\infty} \frac{D_t}{(1 + k)^t}$$

(8-1)

[1] John Burr Williams, *The Theory of Investment Value*. Cambridge, Mass.: Harvard University Press, 1938, p. 58.

where P_0 = intrinsic value at time 0

D = cash dividends per share in time periods $1, 2, \ldots, t$

k = discount rate

If the cash dividends are expected to increase at some constant rate g, the cash dividends in any period D_t can be determined by

$$D_t = D_0(1 + g)^t \tag{8-2}$$

where g = constant growth rate

In Equation (8-2), D_0 represents the dollar amount of the dividend in current time period 0. By substituting Equation (8-2) into Equation (8-1), the basic equation for determining the intrinsic value of a share of common stock can be rewritten as[2]

$$P_0 = \frac{D_0(1 + g)^1}{(1 + k)^1} + \frac{D_0(1 + g)^2}{(1 + k)^2} + \cdots + D_t \frac{(1 + g)^t}{(1 + k)^t}$$

$$= \sum_{t=1}^{\infty} \frac{D_0(1 + g)^t}{(1 + k)^t}$$

That can be simplified to

$$P_0 = \frac{D_0(1 + g)}{k - g} \quad \text{or} \quad P_0 = \frac{D_1}{k - g} \tag{8-3}$$

---

[2] *Proof:*

$$P_0 = D_0 \left[\frac{(1 + g)^1}{(1 + k)^1} + \frac{(1 + g)^2}{(1 + k)^2} + \frac{(1 + g)^3}{(1 + k)^3} + \cdots \right] \tag{a}$$

Multiply both sides of Equation (a) by $(1 + k)/(1 + g)$:

$$\frac{(1 + k)}{(1 + g)} P_0 = D_0 \left[1 + \frac{(1 + g)}{(1 + k)} + \frac{(1 + g)^2}{(1 + k)^2} + \cdots \right] \tag{b}$$

Assume that k is greater than g, and subtract Equation (a) from Equation (b).

$$\left[\frac{(1 + k)}{(1 + g)} - 1 \right] P_0 = D_0$$

$$\frac{(1 + k) - (1 + g)}{1 + g} P_0 = D_0$$

$$(k - g) P_0 = D_0(1 + g) = D_1$$

therefore, $P_0 = \dfrac{D_1}{k - g}$

Assume that the Alfred Isaac Company pays a cash dividend of $2.00 per share D_0, and it expected to grow at 10 percent per year g. Further assume that investors can invest in risk-free government securities that provide a yield of 8 percent. Because investing in the Alfred Isaac Company is riskier than investing in government securities, the investors want a risk premium of say 6 percentage points. The method for determining risk premiums will be presented shortly. The total rate that they expect to earn is 14 percent, which is used as the discount rate k. Accordingly, the intrinsic value of the Alfred Isaac Company is

$$P_0 = \frac{D_1}{k - g}$$

$$= \frac{\$2.00}{0.14 - 0.10}$$

$$= \$50.00$$

In the previous example, it was assumed that the dividends would grow at a constant 10 percent per year. This assumption is not applicable to many companies. Companies that are in cyclical businesses, such as steel and copper, may vary the dollar amount of cash dividends that they pay according to business conditions. Dividend policies are also related to the life cycle, which was explained in Chapter 4. During the pioneering and expansion phases of development, companies require large amounts of funds for expansion; consequently, there is little if any left over for cash dividends. During the stabilization phase, companies have sufficient funds to pay or increase their cash dividends. During the declining phase, some companies pay what amounts to liquidating dividends. Accordingly, the intrinsic value of firms whose rates of growth change over time can be determined by Equation (8-4). This equation breaks the stream of dividend payments into two or more growth rates or time periods. Thus g_x is designated as the first growth rate and g_y is the second growth rate. The equation can be expanded to include any combination of growth rates or time periods. By way of illustration, assume that Marla Industries pays an initial dividend D_0 of $1.00 per share. The growth rate of the dividends in each of the next 5 years g_x is expected to be 35 percent. Thereafter, the growth rate g_y is expected to be 10 percent per year. Finally, investors expect a 20 percent return k on their investment. The steps necessary to determine the intrinsic value of Marla Industries are shown in Table 8-1.

$$P_0 = \sum_{t=1}^{N} \frac{D_0(1 + g_x)^t}{(1 + k)^t} + \sum_{t=N+1}^{\infty} \frac{D_N(1 + g_y)^{t-N}}{(1 + k)^t}$$

where g_x = first rate of growth
g_y = second rate of growth   (8-4)

Table 8-1   The Intrinsic Value of Marla Industries

1. Assumptions:
   a. The initial dividend D_0 is $1.00 per share
   b. The discount rate k is 20 percent
   c. The rate of growth in each of the first 5 years g_x is 35 percent
   d. The rate of growth after 5 years g_y is 10 percent per year
2. The present value for the first 5 years:

$$PV = \sum_{t=1}^{N} = \frac{D_0(1+g_x)^t}{(1+k)^t} = \sum_{t=1}^{5} \frac{\$1\,(1+0.35)^5}{(1+0.20)^5} = \$7.20$$

Year	Dividend $\$1.00\,(1+0.35)^t$	X Discount rate = 0.20	= Present value
1	$1.35	0.833	$1.12
2	1.82	0.694	1.26
3	2.46	0.579	1.42
4	3.32	0.482	1.60
5	4.48	0.402	1.80
			$7.20

3. The value at the end of 5 years from dividends thereafter:
   a. Dividend at end of year 5 = $1\,(1+0.35)^5 = \$4.48$

   b. $P_5 = \dfrac{D_5(1+g_y)}{k - g_y} = \dfrac{D_6}{k - g_y}$

   $\quad = \dfrac{\$4.48\,(1+0.10)}{0.20 - 0.10}$

   $\quad = \dfrac{\$4.93}{0.10}$

   $\quad = \$49.30$

4. Present value of stock at end of year 5 (P_5):
   $PV = P_n\,(1+k)^{-n}$
   $\quad = P_5\,(1+0.15)^{-5}$
   $\quad = \$49.30\,(0.497)$
   $\quad = \$24.50$

5. Per-share value of stock today P_0:
   $P_0 = PV$ for first 5 years + present value of stock at end of year 5
   $\quad = \$7.20 + \$24.50$
   $\quad = \$31.70$

The first step is to determine the present value for the first 5 years, during which time the dividends are growing 35 percent per year. At the end of 5 years, the present value of that future stream of dividends is worth $7.20. The next step is to determine the *value* of the security at the end of 5 years. This is the value of the security in years 6 through infinity. During this period, the rate of growth of dividends slowed from 35 to 10 percent per year. The value at the end of 5 years is $49.30, but the *present value* of that amount is only $24.50. The final step is to add the present value for the first 5 years $7.20 to the present value for the remaining years $24.50 to arrive at the intrinsic value of Marla Industries, which is $31.70 per share.

In summary, the dividend-valuation method of determining the intrinsic value of common stock is based on the idea that the present value of a share of common stock is equal to the sum of the future cash dividends discounted at the appropriate rate. Moreover, the discount rate is larger than the growth rate ($k > g$), and the company is going to pay cash dividends now or at some predictable time in the future. If the company is never going to pay cash dividends, other methods of valuation are available. One such method is explained in the next chapter.

CAPITAL-ASSET PRICING MODEL

The effective use of the dividend-valuation model for determining the intrinsic value of a security depends on the correct estimation of the capitalization rate. The capitalization rate k may be considered the minimum rate of return that investors require. The minimum rate of return that investors require on a risk-free security, such as a United States government bond, is called the risk-free rate of return R_f. Because other securities are riskier than United States government bonds, investors want an additional return, called a risk premium, to compensate them for the additional risk. Thus the required rate of return for any common stock is equal to the risk-free rate of return plus a risk premium:

$$
\begin{aligned}
k &= R_f + \text{risk premium} \\
&= R_f + b(k_m - R_f)
\end{aligned}
\tag{8-5}
$$

where k = required rate of return
R_f = risk-free rate of return
b = beta
k_m = rate of return on the market

Equation (8-5) represents the capital-asset pricing model (CAPM) and may be used in the following manner. The concept of the CAPM is explained in terms of the figure presented in Figure 8-1. The vertical axis represents the required rates of return and the horizontal axis represents risk as measured by beta. As noted in Chapter 2, beta is a measure of risk. A beta of 0.5 means that if the returns on the stock market change 10 percent, the returns of that individual security will tend to change by half (5%) of that amount. A beta of 1 suggests the returns will tend to be the same as the returns on the stock market, and a beta of 1.5 suggests that the returns on that security will be 50 percent more volatile

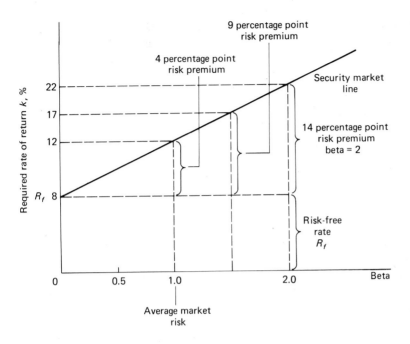

Figure 8-1 Security-market line.

than the returns on the stock market. Thus a low beta suggests low risk and a high beta suggests high risk.

The security-market line represents the relationships between required rates of return for assets and their respective risk as measured by beta. The security-market line is positively sloped, which means that investors require a higher rate of return as risk increases. Since common stocks are risky investments, rational investors require a minimum of the risk-free rate of return plus a risk premium. The risk-free rate is the rate of return on United States government securities and is depicted in Figure 8-1 as 8 percent. If investors expect to take an average risk in the stock market, they should expect an average rate of return. The average rate of return shown here is 12 percent and is determined by finding the average risk on the horizontal axis (beta = 1) and following the dashed line to the vertical axis. Similarly, if the beta were 2, the required rate of return would be 22 percent.

In review, the required rate of return k for any stock can be determined by multiplying the stock's beta by the average market risk premium for that stock, and adding that to the risk-free rate of return. For example, the Alfred Isaac Company had a beta of 1.5 and the required rate of return is

$$k = R_f + b(k_m - R_f)$$
$$= 0.08 + 1.5 \, (0.12 - 0.08)$$
$$= 0.08 + 1.5 \, (0.04)$$
$$= 0.14, \text{ or } 14 \text{ percent}$$

RANKING INVESTMENT PROPOSALS

Strategic planning refers to major action programs that are used by an organization to achieve its mission and goals. Part of the major action programs may involve a large commitment of capital to various investment projects. In the introduction to Chapter 6, it was stated that Lockheed Aircraft Corporation used break-even analysis in evaluating the strategic decision to develop the L-1011 TriStar commercial jet. Had the company used one of the methods described here, their decision might have been different. One independent analyst used the net-present-value method, which will be explained shortly, to evaluate Lockheed's decision to develop L-1011. His study concluded that considerable doubt existed whether a feasible price-sales combination existed at which the L-1011 TriStar program would have been profitable.[3] The use of the net-present-value method of evaluating the L-1011 strategy shed a different light on the project than the break-even analysis. This section of the chapter presents four methods that are useful in deciding which projects to select. The four methods are:

    1 *Payback period*—the number of years required to return the net investment outlay.
    2 *Net present value*—the present value of cash flows discounted at the cost of capital, and less the cost of the investment outlay.
    3 *Profitability index*—the present value of cash flows discounted at the cost of capital, and divided by the investment outlay.
    4 *Internal rate of return*—that rate of interest which equates the present value of cash flows to the investment outlay.

Basic Definitions

Before discussing the four methods of ranking investment proposals, it is necessary to clarify what is meant by the terms "cash flows" and "investment outlay" that were used previously. In addition, several other terms that are used in discussing the methods are defined here.

    Taxes Both cash flows and investment outlay are affected by federal income taxes; so let's mention that item first. The tax effect on the sale or disposition of capital equipment is beyond the scope of this book because of the complexities of the tax laws and their applications. However, the reader must take them into account in order to rank investment proposals accurately. In addition, the tax effects of certain types of expenses that affect both investment outlays and investment returns should be considered. Let t equal the tax rate, which for purposes of illustration is 40 percent. Therefore, the after-tax cost is equal to $(1 - t)$, or 60 percent of the total cost. The savings through a reduction in tax payments are equal to the tax rate t.

---

[3]U. E. Reinhardt, "Break-Even Analysis for Lockheed's TriStar: An Application of Financial Theory," *The Journal of Finance*, September 1973, p. 834.

For Every $1 in Expenses

$1 expense
- tax payments reduced $.40 ($t$)
- actual cost $0.60 ($1 - t$)

Investment Outlay The investment outlay refers to the total amount of *cash* that is required to obtain the asset. To determine the cash outlay, the following items have to be taken into consideration:

1 Payments to the seller
2 Installation costs, which may include site preparation, new facilities, additional power lines, etc.
3 Increases in working capital due to higher inventories, receivables, and other factors
4 Tax effects of the sale or disposition of assets that are being traded in or disposed of in one manner or another

In summary, the investment outlay is a *cash* concept. Therefore, accruals, deferred payments, and other noncash items are not considered part of the investment outlay.

Cash Flows Cash flows are the *expected* net profits after taxes plus depreciation that results from the asset. The annual cash flow R, which can be determined by Equation (8-6), is equal to the change in revenues generated from sales S, less the changes in costs C and depreciation D times the tax factor $(1 - t)$. The result is net profits after taxes, which is added to the change in depreciation. Depreciation is added back into the equation because it is a noncash outlay. Depreciation results in tax savings which are considered in the equation. In addition, Equation (8-6) can be expanded to take into account the salvage value of the assets that are being disposed of and the release of working capital that may result from the acquisition of a new asset. For example, the old asset was sold for scrap for $3500, which means that cash inflows have increased by $3500. In addition, the new asset is so efficient that the "work in progress" inventory has been reduced $8600 per year. Thus the inventory costs can be lowered by that amount. Accordingly, the annual cash flows take into account all the factors that affect cash into and out of a firm. Equation (8-6) can be rewritten as Equation (8-7).

Annual Cash Flow

$$R = (\Delta S - \Delta C - \Delta D)(1 - t) + \Delta D \tag{8-6}$$

$$R = \Delta P + \Delta D \tag{8-7}$$

where Δ = change
P = profits after taxes
D = depreciation charges
S = sales
C = costs
t = tax rate

Types of Investment Proposals   Investment proposals can be classified into two categories: mutually exclusive or independent. Mutually exclusive proposals refer to an "either or" situation where only project X or Y can be selected but not both. For example, one can build a factory or warehouse on the same parcel of land, but both cannot be built on the same site. In contrast, independent proposals have nothing to do with each other. Therefore, two or more independent proposals may be selected if sufficient funds are available.

Payback Period

The payback period is widely used as a method for ranking investment proposals because it is easy to calculate and easy to understand. However, it can provide misleading information and has numerous shortcomings that will be discussed shortly.

The payback period is defined as the number of years required to recover the net investment outlay. The following problem illustrates how to calculate the payback period.

Assume that the net investment required to obtain a new printing machine is $15,000. The cash flows from that machine are:

Years	Cash flows
1	$7000
2	$8000
3	$8500
4	$9000
5	$9500
6	Machine sold for $4000

During the first year, $7000 will be recovered and during the second year, $8000 will be recovered. Thus, by the end of the second year, the entire investment of $15,000 will have been recovered, and the payback period is 2 years.

Advantages   This example demonstrates the principal advantages of the payback period—it is easy to calculate and easy to understand that an investment will be paid back in 2 years. Its simplicity makes it useful as an initial screening device, but beyond that it has some serious shortcomings.

Disadvantages   The first disadvantage of this method is that it ignores returns beyond the payback period. In the example that was used, an additional $31,000 was earned beyond the payback period. Second, the payback period does not take into account the time value of money. Expected returns in the first year are weighed equally with expected returns in future years. However, we know from the previous chapter that $1000 received today is worth more than $1000 received 1 year from now. Third, the payback period does not take into account the costs of financing the investment. Finally, the payback period measures *time*. Stockholders and managers are interested in profits, not time.

Net Present Value

Net present value is the most useful of the capital budgeting techniques. It overcomes the shortcomings of the payback method, it is relatively easy to calculate, and it can be "modified" to take risk into account. Net present value (NPV) is defined as the present value of cash flows discounted at the cost of capital, less the cost of the investment outlay. The cost of capital, or the required rate of return k, may be determined by using the capital-asset pricing model that was explained previously. NPV can be determined by solving Equation (8-8).

Net Present Value

$$\text{NPV} = \left[\frac{R_1}{1+k} + \frac{R_2}{(1+k)^2} + \cdots + \frac{R_n}{(1+k)^n} \right] - I$$

$$= \sum_{t=1}^{n} \left[\frac{R^t}{(1+k)^t} \right] - I \tag{8-8}$$

where R = cash flow
k = cost of capital
I = initial cost of the investment outlay
n = expected life of the investment

Two problems are presented here to illustrate the use of this equation and the present-value concepts that were discussed in the previous chapter. The first problem demonstrates the calculation when expected returns are even in every year. Project A cost $125,000 and is expected to return $25,000 per year for the next 9 years. The cost of capital is 10 percent. The NPV of this investment is calculated by multiplying the cash flow ($25,000) by the interest factor (5.759), which is the present value of an annuity at 10 percent for 9 years. The annuity interest factor can be used because the expected returns are the same size in each year. Next, the product of these two items is subtracted from the investment outlay, and the NPV investment proposal A is $18,975.

Assumptions:

$$I = \$125{,}000$$
$$R = \$\ 25{,}000$$
$$n = 9$$
$$k = 0.10$$

$$NPV = \sum_{t=1}^{9} \frac{\text{Expected}}{\text{returns}} \times \frac{\text{Interest}}{\text{factor}} - \frac{\text{Investment}}{\text{outlay}}$$

$$= \quad \$25{,}000 \ \times \ 5.759 \ - \ \$125{,}000$$
$$= \$18{,}975$$

The second problem demonstrates how to calculate the NPV for investment proposals that have uneven cash flows in every year. The difference between this problem and the previous one is that the present value is calculated for every year when the cash flows are uneven. Two investment proposals, C and D, are considered in this problem. Both require an investment outlay of $10,000 and both have a cost of capital of 10 percent. As shown in Table 8-2, the cash flows for each year are multiplied by the present-value interest factor and then summed. Then the cost of the investment outlay is subtracted to obtain the NPV.

Timing of Returns This problem also demonstrates the importance of *timing* of cash flows. Project C can be considered a "long-term" investment because the largest cash flows are expected in the latter years of the project. In contrast, project D can be considered "short-term" because the largest cash flows occur during the first few years.

Figure 8-2 shows the net-present-value profiles for both projects. The profiles are the relationships between the project's NPV at various discount rates.

Table 8-2 Net Present Value for Projects C and D

	Project C			Project D		
Year	Cash flows	Interest factor at 10%	Present value	Cash flows	Interest factor at 10%	Present value
1	$1,000	0.909	$ 909.00	$8,500	0.909	$ 7,726.50
2	2,000	0.826	1,652.00	3,000	0.826	2,478.00
3	4,000	0.751	3,004.00	1,500	0.751	1,126.50
4	8,000	0.683	5,464.00	500	0.683	341.50
			PV = $11,029.00			PV = $11,672.50
	Less investment outlay I = −10,000.00					$-I$ = −10,000.00
			NPV = $ 1,029.00			NPV = $ 1,672.50

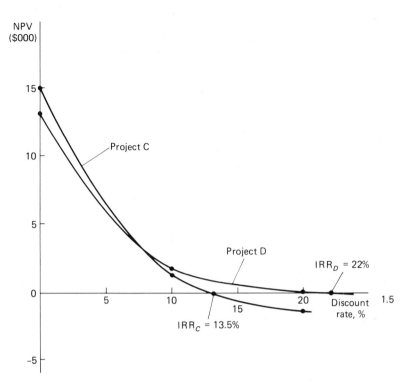

Figure 8-2 Net-present-value profiles for projects C and D.

The profile shows that project C is more responsive or "sensitive" to changes in the discount rate than project D. In other words, if the discount rate increases substantially, project C will lose more (have a lower NPV) than project D. This suggests that investments that are short-term in nature will be more attractive when the cost of capital is high, and investments that are long-term in nature will be more attractive when the cost of capital is low. Figure 8-2 also shows the internal rates of return for projects C and D. The internal rate of return will be explained shortly.

Another type of timing problem occurs when comparing investments that have different project lives. For example, project J has an expected life of 5 years and project K has an expected life of 10 years. One solution to this problem is to develop "replacement chains" so that the maturity of both proposals is the same. This is accomplished by finding the lowest common denominator for the number of years. In this case, the lowest common denominator is 10 years; so the expected returns from project J can be extended another 5 years. If the projects have expected lives of 9 and 13 years, the lowest common denominator is 117 years. Since it does not seem reasonable to extend the life of both investment projects that far into the future, one may select a terminal year that is reasonable. To some extent, the selection of the terminal year depends on the level of the discount rate. For example, if the discount rate is high, say 20 percent, the expected returns 25 years from now will be multiplied by 0.010, which will have a minimal impact on the total value. However, if the discount rate is low, say 4 percent, the cash flows 25 years from now will be multiplied by 0.375, which can have a significant impact on the total value. Therefore, one has to use sound judgment in selecting the terminal year.

Advantages As previously noted, the NPV has advantages that make it particularly useful. First, unlike the payback period, it takes into account the time value of money. Second, the fact that the cost of capital is used as the discount rate gives explicit recognition to the costs of financing and the rate of return required by stockholders. Third, the NPV method gives a dollar amount as an answer. Stockholders and managers are more interested in "dollars" than in "time" or "percent returns." For example, most managers would rather have $10,000 than a 50 percent return on a $19,000 investment.

Finally, the NPV method can be modified to take risk into account. Some investment proposals are riskier than others. Therefore, one can substitute a "risk-adjusted discount rate" or "hurdle rate" for the cost of capital. For example, let's say that the cost of capital is 10 percent and a very risky project is under consideration. Management wants a risk premium of 6 percent in the first year and one additional percentage point in each of the next 10 years. Therefore, the risk-adjusted discount rate will be 16 percent (0.10 + 0.06) in the first year, 17 percent in the second year, etc.

Disadvantages On the other side of the coin, some potential disadvantages are associated with this method. First, it is assumed that funds are reinvested at the cost of capital. As noted previously, a reinvestment-rate assumption is assumed any time that one deals with compound interest or its variants. Therefore, the disadvantage of not reinvesting at the assumed rate applies to *all* the discounted cash flow techniques. The second disadvantage is that the cost of capital is assumed to remain constant. However, this fault can be corrected by making appropriate adjustments to the discount rate whenever changes are expected to occur. In spite of these limitations, the NPV method is one of the primary techniques used to rank investment proposals.

Ranking Criteria The following criteria can be used for ranking investment proposals:

1 By single independent investment proposals.
     Accept the proposal if NPV is positive.
     Reject the proposal if NPV is negative.
2 By multiple independent investment proposals.
     Accept proposals with the highest NPVs. If there is capital rationing, the NPV method may give results that do not maximize the value of

the firm. Therefore, such projects should be ranked by the profitability index, presented next.

3 By mutually exclusive projects.

Accept the project with the highest NPV.

Profitability Index

The profitability index is sometimes called a benefit/cost ratio. It measures the profit per dollar of investment, and it is useful when comparing investment proposals where the investment outlays are of about the same magnitude. The profitability index PI is defined as the present value of expected returns discounted at the cost of capital divided by the investment outlay. The equation for the profitability index is

Profitability Index

$$PI = \sum_{t=1}^{n} \frac{R_t}{(1 + k)^t / I} \tag{8-9}$$

Because this method is so closely related to the NPV method just discussed, no sample problem is given to demonstrate how it is calculated. Nevertheless, it should be pointed out that the profitability index does not give an answer expressed in dollar amounts. When the revenues exceed the costs, the PI will be greater than 1. If this method is used for ranking investment proposals, the proposal with the largest number should be selected first. If the expected returns are less than the costs, the PI will be less than 1.

Internal Rate of Return

The internal rate of return is another popular method for ranking investment proposals. Computing the internal rate of return is more tedious than computing net present value. However, many firms have computer programs that eliminate the trial-and-error process that one must do in order to calculate the internal rate of return manually. Nevertheless, we will work a problem to demonstrate how the internal rate of return is calculated.

The internal rate of return IRR is defined as that rate of interest i which equates cash flows to the investment outlay.[4] The equation for the IRR is

[4] The IRR may also be defined as that rate of interest which will cause the sum of the cash flows less the investment outlay to equal zero. The equation for this formulation is

$$\sum_{t=1}^{n} \frac{R_t}{(1 + i)^t} - I = 0$$

Notice that this is basically the same formulation as the NPV [Equation (8-8)]. Thus the IRR is that rate of discount which causes the NPV to equal zero. See Figures 8-2 and 8-3 for a graphical presentation of this concept. Note that when the NPV = 0, the internal rate of return i and discount rate k are equal.

Internal Rate of Return

$$I = \frac{R_1}{1+i} + \frac{R_2}{(1+i)^2} + \cdots + \frac{R_n}{(1+i)^n}$$

$$= \sum_{t=1}^{n} \frac{R_t}{(1+i)^t} \tag{8-10}$$

where i = internal rate of return
I = initial cost of the investment outlay
R = cash flows

Keep in mind that the equation is solved for i = the interest rate that equates the expected returns R to the investment outlay I.

Trial-and-Error Method To illustrate the use of the equation, refer to Table 8-3, which shows the cash flows for 3 years for investment project L, and the investment outlay, which is $49,090. The first step in solving for the IRR is to make an educated guess at the appropriate rate of interest. If that interest rate results in a total value that is less than the investment outlay, try a lower interest rate next. Using a lower discount rate raises the total value. Similarly, if the interest rate that was used resulted in a total value that was too high, try a slightly higher interest rate. The trial-and-error process is continued until the solution is found.

Table 8-3   IRR of Project L

Assumptions:
Cash flows
R_1 = $17,000
R_2 = $21,000
R_3 = $28,000
I = $49,090

Solution:
(Cash flows X interest factors) = investment outlay

	Interest factors		
Cash flow X **16%**		**14%**	**15%**
R_1 = $17,000 0.862 = $14,654		0.877 = $14,909	0.870 = $14,790
R_2 = $21,000 0.743 = $15,603		0.769 = $16,149	0.756 = $15,876
R_3 = $28,000 0.641 = $17,948		0.675 = $18,900	0.658 = $18,424
Total value $48,205		$49,958	$49,090 = Investment outlay

Sixteen percent is the first interest rate that was selected in the problem. The cash flows discounted at 16 percent result in a total value of $48,205, which is less than the $49,090 investment outlay. Therefore, one should try a lower interest rate next. When the cash flows were discounted at 14 percent, the total value amounted to $49,958, which is more than the investment outlay. Since 16 percent produced results that were too low and 14 percent produced results that were too high, try 15 percent. When the cash flows are discounted at 15 percent, they are equal to the investment outlay. Thus the internal rate of return is 15 percent.

Advantages The advantages of the IRR are that it takes the time value of money into account and provides the compounded rate of return on an investment. The fact that it does not take the costs of financing into account can also be an advantage when the cost of capital is rising. Recall that the NPV method assumed a constant cost of capital.

Disadvantages One disadvantage of this method is the trial-and-error process that one must use to determine the IRR. Another disadvantage is that because the IRR is an interest rate, it does not reflect the size or the scale of the various investment proposals. In addition, the IRR and the NPV may result in different ranking for mutually exclusive investments. More will be said about this topic shortly. Finally, the reinvestment-rate assumption must be considered. This method assumes that funds are reinvested at the IRR.

Ranking Criteria The following criteria can be used for ranking investment proposals by the IRR method:

1 Single independent investment proposals.
> Accept the proposal if IRR exceeds the cost of capital or some acceptable hurdle rate. If the IRR were less than the cost of capital, the NPV would be negative and the value of the firm would be reduced. Reject the proposal if the IRR is less than the cost of capital.

2 Multiple independent investment proposals.
> Accept proposals with the highest IRR.

3 Mutually exclusive projects.
> Accept the investment proposal with the highest IRR.

Some Possible Conflicts

The NPV, PI, and IRR will lead to the same decisions when ranking independent investment proposals. However, under some conditions, the IRR and PI ranking may differ from NPV ranking when dealing with mutually exclusive investment proposals. The two basic conditions that contribute to different rankings are (1) scale effects—the investment outlay of one project is substantially larger than the other project, and (2) timing effects—where the largest cash flows of one project occur during the early years and the cash flows of the other project occur during the later years. Consider the following problem that illustrates the conflicting results associated with differences in scale. The life of both projects M and N is 1 year and the cost of capital is 10 percent. In this example, the size of the investment outlay of project M is one-half the size of the outlay for project N. The data reveal that project M has the highest IRR, 20 percent, and project N has the highest NPV, $15. Which project should be selected?

Project	Investment outlay I	Expected return R	PV at 10%	NPV, $PV - I$	IRR
M	$100	$120	$109	$ 9	20%
N	$200	$236	$215	$15	18%

The net-present-value profiles for projects M and N are shown in Figure 8-3. Whenever the crossover point in such a profile is greater than the cost of capital, the NPV and IRR will give conflicting rankings.

Net Terminal Value   Such conflicts can be resolved by calculating the *net terminal value* NTV. The net terminal value is the difference between total cash flows ($\sum_{t=1}^{n} R_t$) and the compounded sum of the investment outlay at some specified rate of interest for n years $[I(1 + i)^n]$. For example, the net terminal values for projects L and M are $10 and $16, respectively. Project M should be selected because it has the highest NTV.

Project	Expected returns for 1 year	Less	Compounded sum = NTV of I at 10%
L	$120		$100(1.10) = $110 = $10
M	$236		$200(1.10) = $220 = $16

Alternately, one can resolve the conflicting rankings by asking whether reinvestment at the cost of capital or the IRR is the most appropriate. When there is no constraint on the amount of capital that is available for investments, and the cost of capital is expected to remain constant, the correct decision is to assume that funds are reinvested at the cost of capital. However, when there is capital rationing and the cost of capital is rising, the correct decision is to use the IRR. However, one can still use the cost of capital *if* it is adjusted to take the higher costs into account.

Multiple Solutions   Another situation that can create conflicting rankings is when the IRR gives multiple solutions. Normally, investment outlays are made at the beginning of a project, and it is followed by a series of positive net cash

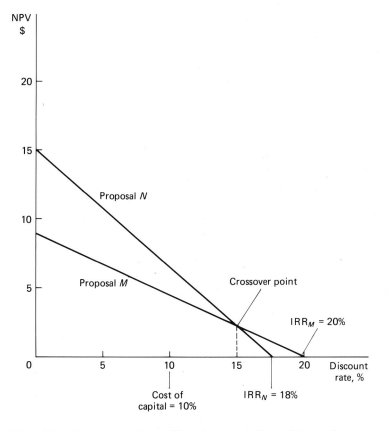

Figure 8-3 Net-present-value profiles of proposals M and N.

flows. However, certain types of projects require large expenditures throughout the life of the investment that may cause negative cash flows later on. For example, the engines on airliners have to be replaced after they have been used for so many hours. Strip coal mines are another example because they have to be filled in and the land restored after the coal has been removed. In such cases, one must use sound judgment and select the most reasonable rate of return. If the most reasonable IRR conflicts with the NPV, the issue can be resolved by calculating the net terminal value or deciding which of the two reinvestment rates is best.

CONCLUSION

In review, this section of the chapter examined four methods of ranking investment proposals or strategic decisions. The payback period is widely used because it is easy to calculate and understand. However, it has serious faults that are overcome by the other methods that were examined.

Net present value is the discounted cash flow technique that has the fewest shortcomings and is favored by the author. It takes the time value of money into account, considers financing costs, and is relatively easy to calculate. It assumes that funds are reinvested at the cost of capital. This, of course, implies that the user knows the cost of capital or at least a "hurdle" rate that is higher than the cost of capital. Finally, NPV gives an answer expressed in dollars, instead of time, an index, or a percentage return.

The profitability index is related to NPV because the expected returns are discounted at the cost of capital. However, the PI lacks the flexibility of NPV, and the answers are expressed as an index. Nevertheless it is useful in determining the profit per dollar of investment in certain situations.

The internal rate of return is the most widely used technique for ranking investment proposals. It is difficult to calculate unless one has a computer that is programmed to do so, and the answer is expressed as an interest rate. This method assumes that funds are reinvested at the IRR. Under some circumstances, the IRR will give rankings that differ from the other methods when ranking mutually exclusive proposals. The key to deciding which ranking is correct lies in the reinvestment-rate assumption. Which rate—the cost of capital or the IRR—is more realistic?

QUESTIONS[†]

1 Assume that a company is considering making a strategic investment in a project that will have the following cash flows and cost:
    Year 1. $ 8 million
    Year 2. $10 million
    Year 3. $15 million
  If the investment outlay for this project is $24.831 million and the firm's cost of capital is 16 percent, should the firm accept or reject the project?
2 Calculate the internal rate of return for the project.
3 If you had to choose between two projects, one having an IRR of 21 percent and the other having a NPV of $3.5 million, which would you select? Why?
4 What are the advantages of NPV?
5 What are the advantages of IRR?

BIBLIOGRAPHY

Bell, David E., Ralph L. Keeney, and Howard Raiffa. *Conflicting Objectives in Decisions*. New York: John Wiley & Sons, Inc., 1978.
Bierman, Harold, Jr., and Seymour Smidt. *The Capital Budgeting Decision*. New York: The Macmillan Company, 1975.

[†]Selected solutions at end of book.

Brigham, Eugene F. *Financial Management: Theory and Practice*. Hinsdale, Ill.:
    The Dryden Press, Inc., 1979.
Jean, William H. *Capital Budgeting: The Economic Evaluation of Investment
    Projects*. Scranton, Pa.: International Textbook Company, 1969.
Johnson, Robert W. *Capital Budgeting*. Belmont, Calif.: Wadsworth Publishing
    Company, Inc., 1970.
Levy, Haim, and Marshall Sarnat. *Capital Investment and Financial Decisions*.
    Englewood Cliffs, N.J.: Prentice-Hall, Inc., 1978.
Osteryoung, Jerome S. *Capital Budgeting:* Long-Term Asset Selection, 2d ed.
    Columbus, Ohio: Grid, Inc., 1979.
Van Horne, James C. *Financial Management and Policy*, 4th ed. Englewood
    Cliffs, N.J.: Prentice-Hall, Inc., 1977.
Weingartner, H. Martin. *Mathematical Programming and the Analysis of Capital
    Budgeting Problems*. Chicago, Ill.: Markham Publishing Co., 1967.
Weston, Fred J., and Eugene Brigham. *Managerial Finance*, 6th ed. Hinsdale, Ill.:
    The Dryden Press, Inc., 1978.

Chapter 9

Understanding Models

Models are used in strategic planning to explore alternative scenarios, to answer "what if" questions, and to solve particular problems. This chapter examines several different types of models that are used in the planning process and explains some limitations of models and their uses.

FUNCTION OF MODELS

A model is an abstraction of reality. It is an objective way of presenting details in the form of a physical or conceptual analogy. Models are isomorphs, which means that they have the same structure as the system they represent. Therefore, whenever a relationship holds between two elements of one system, a corresponding relationship will hold between the relationships in the model. This feature makes models useful to planners because they can estimate the impact on the firm of say acquiring a new company without actually making the acquisition. Models can also be used to answer such questions as what shares of the market will we gain if we give easier credit terms and the competition does not do the same?

Most models that are used in the planning process are conceptual, which means that they are in the form of theories, equations, or ideas. There are also physical models like the scale-model aircraft used in wind-tunnel tests, but such physical models are rarely used in the planning process. Conceptual models are divided into two broad categories: descriptive and predictive.

The life cycle that was explained in Chapter 2 is one example of a descriptive model. It explains the general relationships that exist between sales and profits as a product evolves from infancy to maturity. The purpose of this type of model is to provide a better understanding of particular types of problems or strategies. Descriptive models have definite limitations because they are designed to give general insights as opposed to precise answers.

Predictive models are an attempt to give precise answers about future courses of action. Unfortunately, even the most rigorous mathematical models do not generate precise answers all the time. Some mathematical models that are used to forecast the course of the economy represent the best theories and the latest information that is available, but they rarely predict the exact level and composition of economic activity accurately. Nevertheless, they do provide a better understanding of the processes involved in the economic system.

One reason why the economic forecasting models are not precise is that they cannot be used to predict "unique" events that shape the course of the economy. The extremely harsh winter in early 1977 is one such unique event. Because of the severity of the weather, factories closed down and production of goods and services declined sharply in many parts of the country. Along this line, most models are based on historical data that may be of limited value in predicting the future. For example, one would never have discovered airplanes by studying the previous means of transportation.

Another reason for the lack of precision is that the models may be over-aggregated. That is to say, what is true for the parts may not be true for the whole system. This is commonly referred to as the fallacy of composition. Consider total employment in a firm which does not exhibit the same characteristics as an individual employee. The total level of employees may remain constant, but the composition can shift from engineers to accountants and lawyers. Similarly, one may be able to predict the level of economic activity—the gross national product—although internal errors in the model offset each other. For example, an unexpected decline in housing starts was offset by increased exports. The point is that model users should be aware of the problems of aggregation.

Corporate Model

Against this background, consider the corporate planning model that is used by Dayton Power and Light (Figure 9-1). This model reflects virtually every area of the company's operations. It includes kilowatt (kwh) sales, customer growth, peak demand, generating capacity, fuel costs, and other inputs.

The company uses the corporate model in its planning operations. For

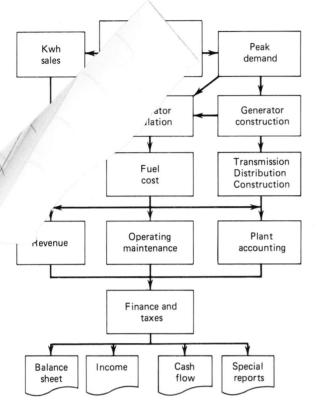

Figure 9-1 Corporate model. (*Source:* Planning Executives Institute.)

example, the model is used to evaluate strategies for obtaining fuel and energy sources to meet their growing demands. Should their strategy be to build additional steam-generating plants or to develop nuclear-power capability? Obviously, the model cannot answer all the questions involved in such a decision, but it provides valuable insights into the impacts of each of these strategies on the firm. Since the model is based on accounting data, the information that it presents is in dollar terms. Thus, for each strategy, the model generates financial statements and special reports.

In addition, Dayton Power and Light has smaller models that provide input into the corporate model. The smaller models are used for generating reports, forecasting, analyzing costs and revenues, and special purposes. For example, the smaller models may be used to determine the impact of a 15 percent increase in fuel costs on company profits or the effect of increased demands on generator capacity.

Specialized Model

The corporate model encompasses all the major areas of the firm and is used for strategic planning and for other purposes. While the corporate model has a large number of applications, some models are developed with one specific job in

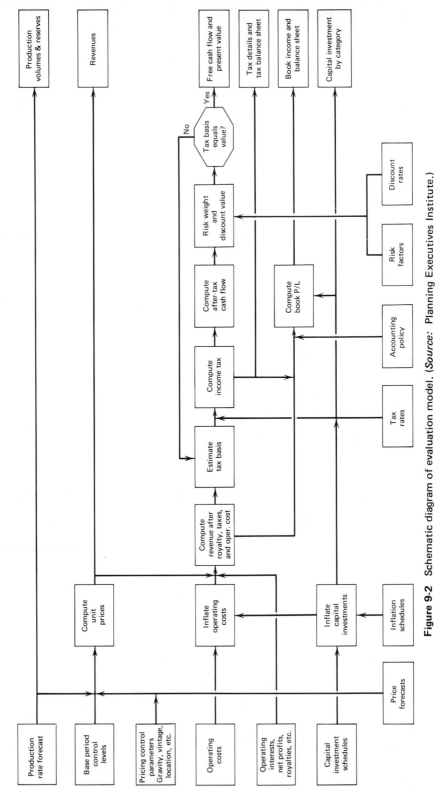

Figure 9-2 Schematic diagram of evaluation model. (*Source:* Planning Executives Institute.)

mind. Consider the specialized model that was used by R. J. Reynolds Industries and their wholly owned subsidiary, American Independent Oil Company (Aminoil) in planning their acquisition of the Burmah Oil Company's interests in the United States. The acquisition was completed in June 1976 for a cash consideration of $422 million, making it the largest cash acquisition in United States corporate history. This model is interesting for two reasons. First, the model was developed for the specific purpose of determining the value of Burmah Oil Company. Because it was developed with a single objective in mind, the model may not be suitable for other purposes.

The second interesting feature of this model is that it used the *net present value* method of project evaluation, which was explained in the previous chapter. A careful examination of Figure 9-2 reveals that most of the input data are used to calculate the after-tax cash flows. After taking risk into account, the after-tax cash flows are discounted to determine the present value of Burmah Oil. Thus Aminoil evaluated the acquisition of Burmah Oil in much the same way that it would evaluate a capital budgeting decision.

SIMULATING THE VALUE OF A FIRM: A CASE STUDY

Computer simulations are widely used to deal with complex problems. Simulation is an analytical technique that involves the use of models to represent the behavior of some real-world situations. For example, the Dayton Power and Light Company uses their corporate model to simulate the effects of disrupted fuel supplies on profits. In order to obtain a better understanding of simulation models, consider the case of Lincoln Industries.

Lincoln Industries' strategy is to grow through acquisition. Lincoln Industries acquired eight companies in the last 5 years and now is considering a ninth merger. The merger candidate is Andrew Manufacturing Company, which makes plastic parts for home appliances. The owner of Andrew Manufacturing wants to retire and is willing to sell controlling interest in the company. David Earl, who is president of Lincoln Industries, is interested in Andrew Manufacturing and wants to determine how much the manufacturing company is worth before pursuing the matter further. This section explains how David Earl used a financial model and a Monte Carlo simulation technique to help him determine the value of Andrew Manufacturing Company.

The Financial Model

The financial model that David Earl used in the simulation is presented in Table 9-1. Some models are complex and consist of hundreds of equations and variables. The one that was used to determine the value of Andrew Manufacturing is relatively simple and consists of seven variables.

Variables The numbers listed below correspond to the item numbers listed in Tables 9-1 and 9-2.

Table 9-1   The Model

$$V = \sum_{t=1}^{n} \frac{Q_0 (1 + g)^t\, P_{mw}}{(1 + k)^t}$$

Item number

1		Total units sold in the *market* area in the base year Q_0
2	times	compound growth rate of unit sales g
3	times	duration of the investment n
4	times	price per unit P
5	equals	total sales in the market for all years considered
	times	market share of the firm m
6	equals	total sales of the firm for all years considered
	times	net income as percent of sales w
7	equals	net income for the firm
	times	present-value factors for every year k
	sum	equals total value of the firm V

    1   The first variable is the total number of *units* sold in the relevant market in the *base* year Q_0. In this case, David Earl used data from government sources to estimate the total number of home appliances that were sold last year in the United States. The relevant market in this case is the United States. David had information from Andrew Manufacturing Company about the number of plastic parts used in each type of home appliance. Therefore, by using both the government data and the information about the number of plastic parts in each type of appliance, David was able to calculate total unit sales for the industry. He recognized that the calculation was not precise. But more will be said about this point when the parameters of the model are discussed shortly.

    2   The compound growth rate of industry sales g is the second variable. David used information from the *U.S. Industrial Outlook*, which is published by the U.S. Department of Commerce, to determine the growth rate of the industry. He also used a variety of trade publications.

    3   The duration of the investment n is the third variable. Investments can be viewed as long-term or short-term. In either case, the number of years must be specified. David considered Andrew Manufacturing a long-term investment.

    4   Price per unit P is the fourth variable. When the total number of units sold is multiplied by the price per unit, the resulting number is the total dollar volume of sales for the entire industry. Keep in mind that this calculation and all the other calculations are made for every year that is being considered.

    5   Market share of the firm m is the fifth variable. When the market share of the firm is multiplied by the total dollar volume of sales for the entire industry, the resulting figure is the total dollar sales for the firm.

    6   The next step is to determine the profitability of the firm. This is accomplished by multiplying the sixth variable—net income as a percent of sales w—by the total sales for the firm.

    7   The final variable is the discount rate k. This is the interest rate that investors use to "capitalize" earnings. It was determined by using the capital-

Table 9-2 The Parameters

Item number	Range of values		
	Minimum	Most likely	Maximum
1 Units (millions)	100.000	150.000	200.000
2 Compound growth rate	0.020	0.110	0.180
3 Number of years	10.000	20.000	30.000
4 Price per unit	0.410	0.600	0.790
5 Market share	0.010	0.040	0.100
6 Net income as percent of sales	0.040	0.060	0.100
7 Discount rate	0.035	0.055	0.090

asset pricing model that was explained in the previous chapter. When the net income is discounted by the appropriate rate, the values for each year are summed to give the total value of the firm V.

Parameters The parameters listed in Table 9-2 are the actual numbers that David Earl used in the model. Note that there are three sets of numbers: (1) the minimum value, (2) the most likely value, and (3) the maximum value. As mentioned earlier, David knew that his calculations were not precise. Nevertheless, he believed that 150 million units was the most likely total number of units sold in relevant markets by all firms. Based on his sources of information, he also determined that the minimum sales were 100 million units and the maximum were 200 million units. Similarly, he estimated a minimum, maximum, and most likely value for each of the remaining variables. The values for all the variables were used in the simulation.

Simulation

A simulation refers to constructing a model that represents reality and then using the model to draw conclusions about a real-life problem. A *Monte Carlo* simulation was used to determine the value of the Andrew Manufacturing Company. The simulation is called Monte Carlo because there is an element of gambling in it. This is so because the *value* of each variable that was used in running the model was selected at *random* from the range of values given in the parameters. Moreover, probability distributions representing the likelihood of occurrence of each value have an assumed shape. Figure 9-3 shows four types of probability distributions. The *uniform distribution* assumes that all values have an equal opportunity of being selected. Therefore, 100 million units of sales has a likelihood of being selected equal to that of 150 million or 200 million units. The *triangular distribution* and the *normal distribution* assume that the values are more or less normally distributed about the most likely value. Therefore, the largest number of values will be selected from the center part of the range of values and fewer will be selected from the upper and lower ends of the distribution. The *beta distribution* can be used when the values are highly skewed.

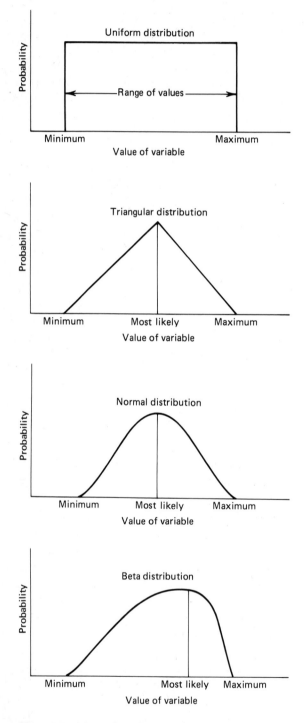

Figure 9-3 Selected types of distributions.

The *triangular distribution* is the easiest one to use because one has only to select the minimum, maximum, and most likely values, such as those shown in Table 9-2, and the computer does the rest of the work. Moreover, there is usually very little difference between the *average* values determined by using the different types of probability distributions. The difference is seen mainly in the high and low estimates that can be obtained. In other words, the extreme values may differ by using the different probability distributions, but the average values will be about the same.

David Earl ran the entire simulation model 500 times and used a triangular probability distribution for each of the variables. He found that 100 runs was not sufficient to take into account all possible random combinations of the variables. At the other end of the spectrum, 1000 runs proved to be excessive. Therefore, he used 500 runs as a reasonable compromise.

The outcome of the 500 runs is presented in the form of a cumulative probability distribution (see Figure 9-4). The cumulative distribution is interpreted in the following manner. Twenty percent of the time, Andrew Manufacturing

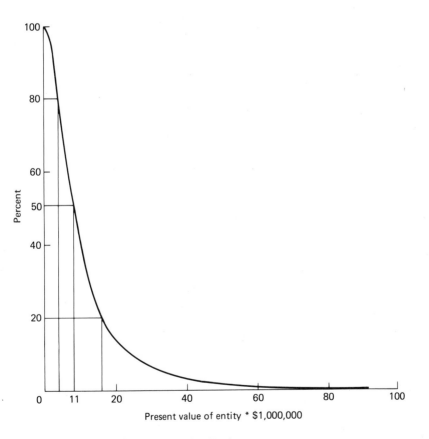

Figure 9-4 Cumulative probability distribution.

Company had a value of $15 million or more, 50 percent of the time the value exceeded $11 million, and 80 percent of the time it exceeded $5 million. The maximum value that was obtained was about $91 million. Based upon this information, David concluded that the *average* value of the firm was $11 million. His bid for the stock was substantially under that figure, and he got it.

The point of this part of the chapter is to demonstrate the use of one type of simulation. The Monte Carlo technique was used to determine the value of a firm. However, that technique and other models can be used to solve a wide variety of problems. The World Bank used a simulation technique to study the replacement of a two-berth, deep-water port in Mogadiscio, Somalia.[1] Simulations are also used in working-capital management and economic forecasting.[2] They are a powerful tool that one can use to answer "what if" questions.

The Limits of Simulations

At a recent seminar on corporate planning and modeling, Dr. Martin Shubik, a noted authority on the subject, presented a listing of when simulations should and should not be used.[3] Although his comments were based on a study made for the Department of Defense, they have their counterparts in the business community. Accordingly, simulations should be used when:

1 It is impossible or extremely costly to observe certain processes in the real world.
2 The observed system is too complex to be described by mathematical equations.
3 No straightforward or analytical technique exists for solution of the appropriate mathematical equations.
4 It is either impossible or very costly to obtain data for more complicated models representing the system.

Simulations should not be used when:

1 Simpler techniques are available.
2 The model is extremely sensitive to minor changes in the data or is not sensitive to any change in the data.

[1]Louis Y. Pouliquen, *Risk Analysis in Project Analysis*, World Bank Staff Occasional Papers No. Eleven. Baltimore, Md.: The Johns Hopkins Press, 1975.
[2]David B. Hertz, "Risk Analysis in Capital Investments," *Harvard Business Review*, 42, January–February 1964, pp. 95–106. "Investment Policies That Pay Off," *Harvard Business Review*, 46, January–February 1968, pp. 96–104.
Kryzanowski, Lawrence, Lusztig, and Schwab, "Monte Carlo Simulation and Capital Expenditure Decisions—A Case Study," *The Engineering Economist*, 18, fall, 1972, pp. 31–48.
[3]Dr. Martin Shubik, "Simulations and Models in the Department of Defense: A Critical Survey of Utilization," *Proceedings from the Fourth Annual Symposium on Corporate Planning and Modeling*, sponsored by SSI, San Francisco, Aug. 19, 1977.

3 The objectives of the study are not clear.

4 Short-term deadlines must be met.

5 The problems are sufficiently unimportant that simulation cannot be cost-effective.

Many of these comments apply to the use of models in general.

ADDITIONAL USES OF MODELS

Dr. Shubik went on to say that most of the models used by the Department of Defense were used for solving particular types of problems such as evaluating new technology and the "product mix" of weapons and personnel. In addition, he discovered four other uses of models that are probably found in many business concerns. He used the word models to include models, simulations, and games. Games are problem-oriented exercises that employ human participants.

Purpose 1. Models are used for scientific window dressing. People who favor a particular project may present a model that "proves" that their pet project is superior to other projects. However, given the correct assumptions, time, and money, a model can be built to prove almost anything.

Purpose 2. Models are used to employ personnel and utilize money that might be withdrawn if the appropriations are not used. Managers in many types of bureaucracies know that they must spend their entire budget because they may receive less in the following year if they fail to do so. Thus the astute manager can always find ways to rewrite computer programs that will "make work" for the computer people.

Purpose 3. Models can be used as a delaying tactic in putting off a decision.

Purpose 4. The final purpose is an after-the-facts justification of the model. A lot of time and money was spent on the model, and it did not work. Nevertheless the wasted time and money can be justified on the following grounds: (*a*) a great deal was learned about the sources of information, and (*b*) the experience gained here can be applied to other problems.

CONCLUSION

Models are useful tools when they are used properly. They can be used to solve problems and gain useful insights that may differ significantly from common intuitive understanding. Model users should keep the following points in mind..

1 Models are designed with a particular purpose in mind.

2 Models must be cost-effective. It does not make sense to build a $100,000 model to solve a $15,000 problem. Moreover, many types of worthwhile models can be acquired from software companies at relatively low cost.

3 Models require a good data base.

4 The predictive ability of models is limited by a variety of factors, including (*a*) the theory and the model may not be precise, (*b*) the data that are used in the model are of poor quality, and (*c*) one cannot predict unique events.

5 Finally, models can be used as a political tool as well as an analytical tool.

QUESTIONS†

1 The life cycle is a descriptive model that has a wide variety of uses. Assume that you have been asked to project the advertising expenses and market-research expenses for a new product over its life cycle. Fill in the blank spaces in Figure 9-5 with your estimates of the level of expenditures. You may use terms like high and low to describe the level of expenses.

2 Some of the variables in models are classified as *endogenous* or *exogenous*. Endogenous means that the variable is influenced by forces inside the system. The weather, for example, may be an exogenous variable for corporate planning. Examine the corporate model shown in Figure 9-1 and list two exogenous variables.

3 How does the financial model for determining the value of a firm that is presented in Table 9-1 differ from the dividend-valuation model that was presented in the previous chapter?

† Selected solutions at end of book.

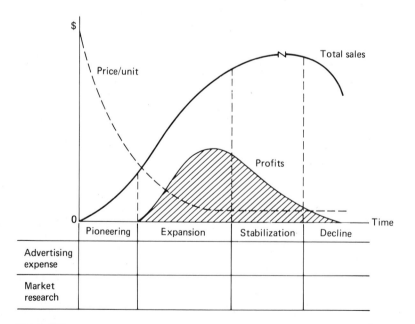

Figure 9-5

4 Use Figure 9-4 to determine the following:
   a What is the probability that Andrew Manufacturing is worth $5 million?
   b What is the probability that Andrew Manufacturing is worth $16 million?
5 What are the major factors limiting the use of corporate planning models?

BIBLIOGRAPHY

Boulden, James B. *Computer Assisted Planning Systems.* New York: McGraw-Hill Book Company, 1975.

Gershefski, George W. *The Development and Application of a Corporate Financial Model.* Oxford, Ohio: Planning Executives Institute, 1968.

Ishikawa, Akira. *Corporate Planning and Control Model Systems.* New York: New York University Press, 1975.

Miller, Ernest C. *Advanced Techniques for Strategic Planning.* New York: American Management Association, 1971.

Naylor, Thomas H. *The Politics of Corporate Planning and Modeling.* Oxford, Ohio: Planning Executives Institute, 1978.

Pouliquen, Louis Y. *Risk Analysis in Project Analysis,* World Bank Staff Occasional Papers No. 11. Baltimore, Md.: The Johns Hopkins Press, 1975.

Spulber, Nicolas, and Ira Horowitz. *Quantitive Economic Policy and Planning: Theory and Models of Economic Control.* New York: W. W. Norton & Company, Inc., 1976.

Part Four

Strategies for Growth

This book is about strategic planning, and this part of the book deals with various types of strategies. Chapter 10 deals with financial strategies for growth. It explains how financial leverage and dividend policy can influence corporate growth. Chapter 11 is about market strategies for growth; and Chapter 12 is about portfolio theory, a new technique that combines risk and returns to make financial decisions. The final chapter of the book is a case study of The Mead Corporation. It explains the evolution of the strategic-planning process at Mead.

Chapter 10

Financial Strategies for Growth

Some relationships between key financial variables and the phases of the development of the life cycle were presented in Chapters 4 and 5 and are summarized in Figure 10-1. The figure shows that levels of profits, cash dividends, and financial leverage differ during various phases of development of the life cycle. During the expansion phase of the life cycle when a firm's growth is rapid, profits increase, cash dividends tend to be small but increasing, and financial leverage is high. During the stabilization phase of the life cycle when a firm's growth rate slows, profits decrease, cash dividends increase, and financial leverage decreases. These, of course, are generalizations that may not apply to some firms. Nevertheless, the point is that growth, the life cycle, and the financial variables are interrelated. As will be explained in the next chapter, there are some compelling reasons for a firm to grow as rapidly as possible. This chapter demonstrates how firms can alter their growth rates by changing their dividend policies and financial leverage. The issues of growth, dividend policy, and financial leverage are explained in the context of an equation that is developed progressively. The first part of the chapter deals with dividend policies of firms that have no debt. Next, the relationship between growth and debt is explored. Finally, both

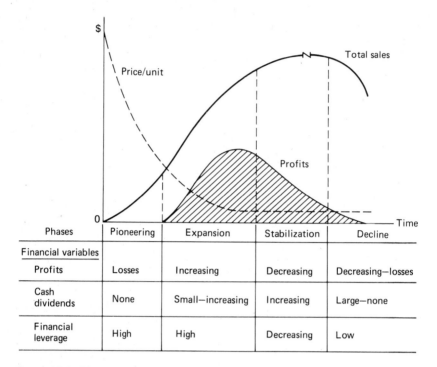

Figure 10-1   The life cycle and key financial variables.

Phases	Pioneering	Expansion	Stabilization	Decline
Financial variables				
Profits	Losses	Increasing	Decreasing	Decreasing—losses
Cash dividends	None	Small—increasing	Increasing	Large—none
Financial leverage	High	High	Decreasing	Low

dividend policy and debt are examined together to demonstrate their combined effects on growth.[1]

GROWTH WITH NO DEBT

The term growth as used here refers to the growth rate of total assets. Let's begin the study of growth by examining a hypothetical firm that has no debt and pays no dividends. Although most firms have some debt, some have little or no debt. For example, debt accounts for only 3 percent of total capital of DeBeers Consolidated Mines, Ltd., a South African mining company. The illustration of a firm with no debt is a reference point that is useful to demonstrate the impact of debt on growth, which will be explained shortly.

When a firm has no debt and pays no dividends, the growth rate of assets g is equal to the rate of return on assets r. Consider the example that is presented in Table 10-1. At the beginning of year 1, the firm had total assets of $100.00. During the year, the firm earned 12 percent ($12.00) on its assets. Since the company pays no dividends or interest, the assets increase by the amount of the

---

[1] The methodology used in this chapter draws on Eugene Lerner and Willard Carleton, *A Theory of Financial Analysis.* New York: Harcourt Brace Jovanovich, Inc., 1966.

Table 10-1 Growth with No Debt or Dividends†

	Years		
	1	2	3
Total assets at the beginning of each year	$100.00	$112.00	$125.44
Debt	0.00	0.00	0.00
Equity	100.00	112.00	125.44
Profit	12.00	13.44	15.05
Total assets at the end of each year	112.00	125.44	140.49
Growth rate of assets, %	12	12	12

†Return on assets $r = 12$ percent.
No taxes
$g = r = 12$ percent

retained earnings and equal $112.00 at the end of the year. The same pattern occurs in the second and third years. The growth rate of the assets during each year is 12 percent because all the earnings are being retained and added to the firm's capital. Thus a firm that pays no debt and retains all its earnings will grow at the same rate as the return on its assets.

Let's relax the restriction about not paying dividends and assume that the firm pays a dividend that amounts to 40 percent of its profit. The remaining 60 percent is retained earnings. As shown in Table 10-2, the total assets are $100.00 at the beginning of the first year. The company earns 12 percent ($12.00), but 40 percent ($4.80) of that amount is paid out as dividends. The remaining $7.20 is retained earnings and the growth rate of the assets is reduced to 7.2 percent. If the same pattern exists in the next 2 years, the growth rate of assets is 7.2 percent. Had the firm paid out 80 percent of its profit in dividends, the growth rate of assets would have been 2.4 percent.

Table 10-2 Growth with No Debt and 40 Percent Dividend Payout†

	Years		
	1	2	3
Total assets at the beginning of each year	$100.00	$107.20	$114.92
Debt	0.00	0.00	0.00
Equity	100.00	107.20	114.92
Profit	12.00	12.86	13.79
Dividend	4.80	5.14	5.52
Retained earnings	7.20	7.72	8.27
Total assets at the end of each year	107.20	114.92	123.19
Growth rate of assets, %	7.2	7.2	7.2

†Return on assets $r = 12$ percent.
No taxes
$g = br = (0.60)(0.12) = 7.2$ percent

The important point is that the growth rate of assets of a firm with no debt depends on (1) the rate of return on assets r and (2) the proportion of earnings retained by the firm after dividends have been paid b. Specifically, the growth rate of such a firm can be expressed as

$$g = br \qquad\qquad (10\text{-}1)$$

where b and r remain constant through time.

DIVIDEND POLICY

The effects of five dividend policies (indicated by the proportion of retained earnings b) on the growth rates of assets of firms with no debt are shown in Table 10-3. If the rate of return on assets remains unchanged at 12 percent, the growth rate of assets increases as the proportion of earnings retained by the firm increases.

When the firm pays out all its earnings as dividends ($b = 0.00$), the growth rate g is zero. When half the earnings are retained ($b = 0.50$), the growth rate is 6 percent. The maximum rate of growth is achieved when all the earnings are retained ($b = 1.00$). Accordingly, firms that pay no dividends grow at faster rates than those that pay dividends. It also follows that firms that have small dividend payout ratios will grow at a faster rate than those that have large payout ratios. This, of course, assumes that retained earnings are reinvested at the same rate of return on total assets.

What dividend policy is best for stockholders? If stockholders prefer capital gains to dividends, the firm should pay no dividend or a small dividend. If stockholders prefer dividends to capital gains, the question of when they want to receive the dividends becomes important. In the *long run*, stockholders will receive larger dividends by owning firms that retain most of their earnings and have high rates of growth than by owning firms that pay out most earnings and grow at a slower pace. Consider two firms, LoDiv and HiDiv, each earning $2 per share and having a rate return on assets of 12 percent. LoDiv pays a dividend of $0.50 per share, which means that it retains 75 percent of its earnings and the

Table 10-3 Selected Growth Rates

Growth rate g, %	=	Proportion of earnings retained by the firm b	×	Rate of return on assets r
0		0.00		0.12
3		0.25		0.12
6		0.50		0.12
9		0.75		0.12
12		1.00		0.12

growth rate of its assets and dividends is 9 percent. HiDiv pays a dividend of $1.50 per share, which means that it retains 25 percent of its earnings and the growth rate of its assets and dividends is 3 percent. For 19 years, the dividends of HiDiv will be greater than those of LoDiv. In the twentieth year, the dividends of LoDiv will be $2.80 per share compared with the $2.71 per share paid by HiDiv. However, by the twenty-fifth year, the dividends of the LoDiv company will have increased to $4.31 per share compared with dividends of $3.14 per share for the stockholders of the HiDiv company. Thus, after the nineteenth year, the stockholders of the LoDiv company will receive larger cash dividends than the stockholders of the HiDiv company. Most investors would probably prefer HiDiv because they may not want to retain that stock for such an extended period.

In review, dividend policy has important implications for the growth of a firm. If all other things are held constant, a low dividend payout ratio—a high proportion of retained earnings—is associated with high rates of growth. In addition, after a period of years, the stockholders of firms with low dividend payout ratios will receive higher cash dividends than the stockholders of firms with high dividend payout ratios. Equally important, the idea behind rapid growth is to dominate the market. For reasons that will be explained in the next chapter, firms that have the largest volume of sales tend to have the lowest cost per unit and the best opportunities for profit.

GROWTH WITH DEBT

The previous examples assumed that the firms had no debt. Now that assumption is relaxed. However, the firms used in the following examples have constant debt-to-equity ratios. Table 10-4 shows the growth of a firm that is financed equally by debt and by equity and pays no dividends. The debt-to-equity ratio of this firm is 1/1 (50 percent debt/50 percent equity = 1/1). The rate of return on assets r is 12 percent, and the interest rate on the debt is 5 percent. As in the previous examples, total assets at the beginning of the first year are $100.00 and profits are $12.00. The interest payment of $2.50 is deducted from profits before interest in order to obtain profits after interest—$9.50. Since no dividends are paid, the $9.50 profit is retained by the firm as equity. Because the firm maintains a constant debt-to-equity ratio, an additional $9.50 of debt is obtained, and the total new investment in the firm is $19.00. Therefore, the assets are $119.00 at the end of the year and the growth rate of assets is 19 percent. The same process occurs in the following years.

Leverage and Growth

The firm used in Table 10-4 demonstrated that the debt provided financial leverage which increased the growth rate of the firm when earnings increased.

Table 10-4 Growth with Debt but No Dividends[†]

	Years		
	1	2	3
Total assets at the beginning of each year	$100.00	$119.00	$141.60
Debt	50.00	59.50	70.80
Equity	50.00	59.50	50.80
Profit before interest	12.00	14.28	16.99
Interest	2.50	2.98	3.54
Profit after interest	9.50	11.30	13.45
Retained earnings	9.50	11.30	13.45
Additional debt	9.50	11.30	13.45
Total new investment	19.00	22.60	26.90
Total assets at the end of each year	119.00	141.60	168.50
Growth rate of assets, %	19.0	19.0	19.0

[†]Return on assets $r = 12$ percent.
No taxes
$i = 5$ percent
$g = br + (r - i)\dfrac{L}{E}$
$= 1.0(0.12) + (0.12 - 0.05)\dfrac{50}{50} = 19$ percent

The effects of financial leverage on the growth rate of assets g can be demonstrated by using Equation (10-2).[2] This equation is based on Equation (10-1) ($g = br$), but it takes the effect of interest payments $(r - i)$ and leverage (L/E) into account.

$$g = br + (r - i)\frac{L}{E} \tag{10-2}$$

where g = growth rate of assets
    b = proportion of earnings retained by the firm after dividends have been paid
    r = rate of return on assets
    i = interest rate on borrowed funds
    L = liabilities (debt)
    E = equity

As previously noted, the debt-to-equity ratio for the firm used in Table 10-4 is 1/1 and the growth rate of assets is 19 percent.

$$g = br + (r - i)\frac{L}{E}$$

$$= 1.0\,(0.12) + (0.12 - 0.05)\frac{50}{50} = 19 \text{ percent}$$

[2]See Appendix 10B for the derivation of equations.

If the debt-to-equity ratio is increased to 2/1 (100/50 = 2/1), the growth rate of the assets will double.

$$g = 1.0 \ (0.12) + (0.12 - 0.05) \ \frac{100}{50} = 38 \text{ percent}$$

Similarly, increasing the debt-to-equity ratio to 3/1 will increase the rate of growth of assets to 57 percent.

Leverage and EPS

Financial leverage also has a marked effect on earnings per share (EPS). It increases the volatility of the earnings per share and the financial risk of the firm. Both these effects are illustrated in Table 10-5, which shows three companies with different degrees of leverage. The degrees of leverage are indicated by the debt-to-equity ratios. Company A has no financial leverage because it is financed entirely by common stock and has a debt-to-equity ratio of 0/1. Company B is financed equally by debt and common stock and has a 1/1 debt-to-equity ratio. Company C is highly leveraged because 90 percent of its financing comes from debt and it has a 9/1 debt-to-equity ratio. The important parts of the table are the earnings per share, which are calculated in the following manner. Fixed interest payments of $1 per bond are deducted from total earnings and the remainder is divided by the number of shares outstanding. For example, if each company earned $100, their respective stockholders would earn $1 per share. In the case of Company B, for example, $50 would be paid in interest and the remaining $50 would be divided evenly among the 50 shares of stock. If total earnings increased to $200, stockholders of Company A would earn $2 per share, stockholders of Company B would earn $3 per share, and stockholders of Company C would earn $11 per share: ($200 earnings − $90 interest)/10 shares = $11/share.

Table 10-5　Financial Leverage

	Company A	Company B	Company C
Number of shares of stock ($100 each)	100	50	10
Number of bonds ($100 each)	0	50	90
Debt-to-equity ratio	0/1	1/1	9/1
Fixed interest charges ($1 per bond)	0	$50	$90
Total earnings before interest payments	Earnings per Share		
$100	$1	$1	$1
$200	$2	$3	$11
$50	$0.50	$0	Deficit of $40

As long as total earnings are rising, financial leverage has a beneficial effect on earnings per share. However, financial leverage also magnifies the effects of lower earnings on earnings per share. If total earnings fell to $50, Company C would be unable to meet its interest payments. In fact, it would have a deficit of $40 per share. This example demonstrated that leverage is a two-edged sword. When total earnings increased 100 percent, Company C's earnings increased 1100 percent. However, when total earnings declined 50 percent, the highly leveraged Company C was unable to cover its fixed interest changes.

In spite of the fact that financial leverage is a two-edged sword, there are significant advantages to using it as long as the rate of return on assets r is greater than the interest rate on borrowed funds. One advantage that has been demonstrated is that a firm can increase its rate of growth by using leverage. This is important because the leveraged firm may be able to expand its productive capacity at a faster rate than its competitors and obtain a larger market share. Another advantage is that the leveraged firm can accept lower rates of returns on assets and still grow at a rapid rate. On the other side of the coin, increased financial risk may have an adverse effect on the firm's credit standing and share prices.

GROWTH, LEVERAGE, AND DIVIDENDS

The previous discussions focused on growth, leverage, and dividends individually. This section examines various combinations of leverage and dividend policies on the growth rate of assets of three companies, A, B, and C. As shown in Table 10-6, Company A has no financial leverage and has a debt-to-equity ratio of 0/1. Company B has moderate leverage, and Company C is highly leveraged, with debt-to-equity ratios of 1/1 and 9/1, respectively. When all the earnings are paid

Table 10-6   Growth, Leverage, and Dividends[†]

		Company A	Company B	Company C
Debt/equity ratio		0/1	1/1	9/1
Dividend payout ratio %	**Percent of retained earnings**		Growth rate of assets, %	
1.00	0.00	0.00	0.00	0.00
0.75	0.25	3.00	4.25	18.75
0.50	0.50	6.00	8.50	37.50
0.25	0.75	9.00	12.75	56.25
0.00	1.00	12.00	19.00	75.00

†Assume $r = 12$ percent
   $i = 5$ percent

out as dividends—there are no retained earnings—leverage does not affect the growth rate of assets. However, as the dividend payout ratio diminishes (retained earnings increase), leverage has an increasing effect on the growth rates of assets. Thus, when the dividend payout ratio is 0.50, the growth rates ranged from 6 percent for Company A to 37.5 percent for Company C. When all earnings are retained, the maximum rates of growth for companies A, B, and C are 12, 19, and 75 percent, respectively. These numbers demonstrate clearly that companies can alter their rates of growth by changing their leverage and dividend policies.

CONCLUSION

This chapter demonstrated the effects of dividend policies and financial leverage on the growth rates of assets. In general, a dividend policy that requires a small dividend payout ratio and a high debt-to-equity ratio is associated with high growth rates. One advantage of high growth rates is that they may permit the firm to have a competitive edge over other firms that are growing at a slower pace. As will be explained in the next chapter, there are definite advantages to establishing a dominant market share as soon as possible during the pioneering or expansion phases of the life cycle. The disadvantage of higher growth rates that are attributable to financial leverage is the increased financial risk to the firm.

QUESTIONS[†]

1 Which of the following variables has the *most* important influence on the growth of assets?
   a b
   b r
   c i
   d E

2 Using the equation shown at the bottom of Table 10-4, what will happen to the growth rate of the firm if the interest rate charged on the borrowed funds is doubled?

3 Turn to Table 10-5 and calculate the earnings per share if total earnings before interest payments were $400.

4 How does financial leverage differ from operating leverage, which was explained in Chapter 6?

5 Should lease payments and preferred-stock dividends be included when considering the effects of financial leverage on earnings per share?

[†] Selected solutions at end of book.

BIBLIOGRAPHY

Brigham, Eugene F. *Financial Management: Theory and Practice*, 2d ed. Hinsdale, Ill.: The Dryden Press, Inc. 1979.

Growth and Financial Strategies. Boston, Mass.: The Boston Consulting Group, 1971.

Lerner, Eugene M., and Willard T. Carleton. *A Theory of Financial Analysis*. New York: Harcourt Brace Jovanovich, Inc., 1966.

Robichek, Alexander A., and Stewart C. Myers. *Optimal Financing Decisions*. Englewood Cliffs, N.J.: Prentice-Hall, Inc., 1965.

Van Horne, James C. *Financial Management and Policy*, 4th ed. Englewood Cliffs, N.J.: Prentice-Hall, Inc., 1977.

Weston, Fred J., and Eugene Brigham. *Managerial Finance*, 6th ed. Hinsdale, Ill.: The Dryden Press, Inc., 1978.

APPENDIX 10A: Definition of Terms

1 A = assets
2 L = liabilities
3 E = stockholders' equity
4 L/E = debt-to-equity ratio
5 I = interest payments
6 i = interest rate on borrowings

$$i = \frac{I}{L}$$

7 PBT = profit before taxes
8 T = income tax rate

$$T = \frac{\$ \text{ taxes}}{\text{PBT}}$$

9 NI = net income or loss after taxes

$$\text{NI} = (1 - T)(\text{PBT})$$

10 b = percent of net income retained by the firm after dividend payment
11 r = rate of return on assets, sometimes called ROI—return on invested assets

$$r = \frac{\text{PBT} + I}{A}$$

APPENDIX 10B: Development of the Basic Equation

1 By definition, assets equal liabilities plus stockholders' equity.

$$A = L + E \tag{a}$$

2 Profits can be expressed

$$PBT = rA = iL \tag{b}$$

3 Since $A = L + E$ [Equation (a)], profits can also be written as

$$PBT + r(L + E) - iL \tag{c}$$

or $\qquad PBT = \left[r + (r - i) \dfrac{L}{E} \right] E \tag{d}$

4 Profits after taxes, or NI, are

$$NI = (1 - T)(PBT) \tag{e}$$

or $\qquad NI = (1 - T) \left[r + (r - i) \dfrac{L}{E} \right] E \tag{f}$

5 The rate of return on equity is

$$\frac{NI}{E} = (1 - T) \left[(r - i) \frac{L}{E} \right] \tag{g}$$

6 As long as the debt-to-equity ratio L/E remains constant, the company's assets, profits, and dividends will grow at

$$g = b(1 - T) \left[r + (r - L) \frac{L}{E} \right] \tag{h}$$

Alternatively, where there is no debt, g may be expressed

$$g = br \tag{i}$$

if b and r remain constant over time.

Chapter 11

Market and Portfolio Strategies for Growth

This chapter examines market and portfolio strategies and their implications for growth. The chapter is divided into three parts. The first part focuses on four strategies dealing with markets and products. Then the focus shifts to experience curves and their strategic implications. The third part of the chapter examines portfolio strategies and explains the relationships between these strategies and the life cycle and key financial variables.

MARKET STRATEGIES

Four market strategies are presented in the matrix shown in Figure 11-1. The strategies focus on products and markets. The first row of the matrix shows that there are two strategies for firms or other types of organizations that want to grow and remain in their present market. The first strategy is to use the present products and increase market share. The second strategy is to introduce new products into the present market. The second row of the matrix shows two strategies for firms that are willing to enter new markets. The strategies are to

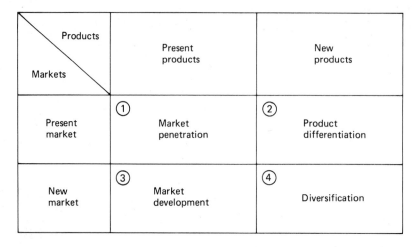

Figure 11-1   Market strategies for growth.

use the present products in the new market and to diversify into other products in the new market.

The four market strategies for growth are demonstrated in the following case of a university that is facing declining enrollment because of demographic factors that stem from a reduction in the birth rate.[1] The fact that a university is used to demonstrate the strategies shows that they can be applied to both profit and nonprofit organizations.

Market Penetration

The first strategy is to gain a larger share of the existing market. The existing market for the university consists of full-time students who are 18 to 24 years old. The increased market penetration can be accomplished in several ways. One method is to send representatives of the university to more high schools and to distant cities in order to reach a larger number of potential students. Another method is to reduce admission standards so that a larger number of students will be "qualified" to enter. However, neither of these methods is satisfactory for the long run because the population of potential students is declining.

Product Differentiation

The second strategy is to offer a different product to the present group of students. The different product could be a better "quality" education because that institution has more noted scholars than competing institutions. Another method is to offer courses that include overseas travel, which some students may

[1]This case is based on a study by Sherry Manning, *Management Strategies for Institutional Growth*, Reprint No. 128, School of Business, the University of Kansas, Lawrence, Kan., 1976.

find attractive. Finally, the university may make extensive use of advanced communications media such as computers, television, audio cassettes, and video tapes. This strategy has the same flaw as the first one. The institution is working harder and harder to maintain its share of a declining market.

Market Development

The third strategy is to offer the present products in new markets. The new markets consist of all potential students other than the traditional 18- to 24-year-olds. For example, many homemakers and people working full time desire more education (i.e., adult education). The new market also includes teaching at different geographic locations. Basically, the idea is to bring education to the people instead of having the people come to the university for an education. Several universities are offering special master degree programs for executives. The courses for the special program are held once or twice a month at key cities located throughout the United States. Many universities offer "extension" courses that are held at off-campus sites. Several offer courses taught on closed-circuit television beamed to students located at remote or rural areas. This strategy has important implications for capital utilization, utilization of existing faculty, site selection, and many other problems that do not exist under the present system. However, the present system cannot cope with declining enrollment; so the institution must change if it is to survive. The new environment is where the university must seek students rather than be sought.

Diversification

The fourth strategy is to diversify into new types of education. For example, the university can offer "continuing education" courses that are designed for the public at large and do not give college credit. In addition, it may establish "certificate" programs. A person completing say five special courses is given a "certificate in management" or a certificate in some other area of interest. This strategy, which is aimed at "nontraditional" students, can produce revenue to support the traditional higher education programs that are being run at a loss.

In review, the matrix shown in Figure 11-1 presents four market strategies for growth in present and new markets. The four strategies are:

1 Increased market penetration
2 Product differentiation
3 Market development
4 Diversification

In the case of the university, the first two strategies may help to increase enrollment in the short run but are not suitable for the long-run strategies because of demographic factors. Therefore, the last two, which are aimed at new markets, appear to be better suited for the long run.

EXPERIENCE CURVES

This section focuses on the relationship among cost, price, and market share. It will be shown that firms that dominate the market tend to have the lowest cost per unit. One reason this is so can be traced back to learning curves. The concept of a learning curve is that the more often someone does something, the better they get at doing it. It makes sense that good tennis players practice more often than poor tennis players. This same idea has some validity in the production of goods and services. Workers learn how to produce goods efficiently as the total volume of production increases. In other words, the cost per unit tends to decline as the volume of output increases. If the cost per unit declines 20 percent every time output doubles, the rate of learning is said to be 80 percent. Figure 11-2 shows an 80 percent learning curve. The curve is plotted on a graph which produces a straight line when the unit cost declines by a fixed percentage each time the cumulative volume doubles. As a general matter, most learning curves range from 70 to 90 percent, which means that the cost per unit declines from 30 to 10 percent every time cumulative output doubles.

In recent years, investigators have expanded the idea of a learning curve into an experience curve.[2] The experience curve encompasses all costs including labor, administrative, capital, marketing, and research. In general, costs per unit of output decline between 10 and 30 percent every time total output doubles. The total accumulated output is called the industry "experience."

Texas Instruments (TI) is one of many companies that make extensive use of learning curves. Specifically, "The learning curve certainly is chapter one in the TI 'bible.' The concept is fundamental to the success of TI's strategy in driving for the leadership position in a high-volume market because the gospel goes, the company with the largest share of the sales has the best opportunity for profit."[3] By way of illustration, TI applied learning curves to its semiconductor business. In 1960, the simplest functional circuit required two transistors and other parts and cost $10. Today, a single silicon chip accommodates 20,000 functions and costs less than 1 cent per function. By 1990, TI estimates that a single chip will contain 10 million or more functions and cost less than one-hundredth of a cent per function.

Some Limitations

The Boston Consulting Group that did the basic work on experience curves points out in *Perspectives on Experience* that cost-volume analysis is a powerful

[2]The pathfinder in this area was the Boston Consulting Group, which published *Perspectives on Experience* in 1968 and *Experience Curves as a Planning Tool* in 1970. Additional information on experience curves was presented by Dr. Subhash C. Jain at the 1977 Annual Meeting of the Planning Executives Institute.

[3]"Texas Instruments Shows U.S. Business How to Surive in the 1980s," *Business Week,* Sept. 18, 1978, p. 68. For information on learning curves in the aircraft industry, see K. Hartley, "The Learning Curve and Its Application to the Aircraft Industry," *Journal of Industrial Economics*, March 1965, pp. 112–118.

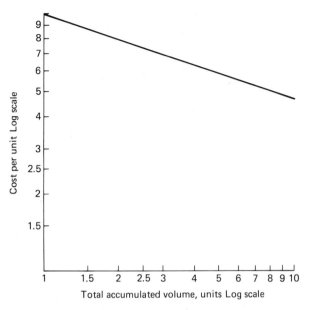

Figure 11-2 80 percent learning and experience curve.

tool that should be considered a means of understanding relationships and not a measuring device. This is so because there are difficulties encountered in defining products and measuring value added and costs. Recognizing that the tool is not perfect, let's see how it can be used.

Cost and Market Share

Experience can be equated with market share when the market shares are relatively constant over time. If costs decline, as the experience curve suggests, the firm that produces the most will have the largest market share and the lowest cost. Figure 11-3 depicts the cost per unit and the accumulated volume for four hypothetical firms A, B, C, and D. Firm D has the greatest total experience (accumulated volume) and the lowest cost per unit. In other words, it has the biggest market share and the lowest cost per unit. Firms C, B, and A have smaller market shares and higher costs. So what?

The significance of the cost/market share relationship is that firms with big market shares tend to have higher returns on investment than firms with small market shares. This is so because the cost per unit of the firms with the big market shares is generally less than the cost per unit of the firms with small market shares. The reasons why the cost per unit are less for the firms with the biggest market shares include learning effects, economies of scale, and technology. With large-scale production, it is possible to spread costs over a sufficiently large number of units of output so that the cost per unit is relatively low. In this way firms such as those in primary metals that require large-scale

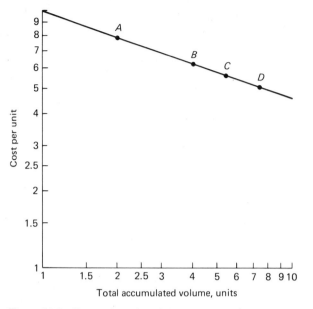

Figure 11-3   Cost and market share.

production may be able to utilize their production capacity more economically than firms with smaller-scale production. Another factor is that the dominant firm may be in better position to afford research and development that can result in design changes and product improvements that reduce costs further.

In summary, cost per unit, market share, and returns on investment are interrelated. Firms with the biggest market shares—the most accumulated experience—tend to have the lowest unit cost. It follows that as the market share increases, the profit margin on sales increases at a more rapid pace. Therefore, market power and profitability frequently go hand in hand, and firms should develop strategies to increase their market shares. However, there are numerous examples of firms that dominate markets and are not profitable. Moreover, there are risks associated with high market shares. Firms that dominate the market are better targets for antitrust suits than firms with a small market share. Similarly, the dominant firms are the most likely targets of consumer groups and regulators. Finally, the cost of obtaining additional market share may not be worth the effort. One must weigh the expected benefits of attaining a higher market share with all the costs associated with attaining that share. Thus the four market strategies that were presented at the beginning of this chapter and summarized in Figure 11-1 may be modified to take these factors into account. For example, strategy 1, increasing market penetration with the present products in the present market, may not be a wise decision if the firm has only a small share of the market and its financial structure (discussed in the previous chapter) is not suitable for rapid growth.

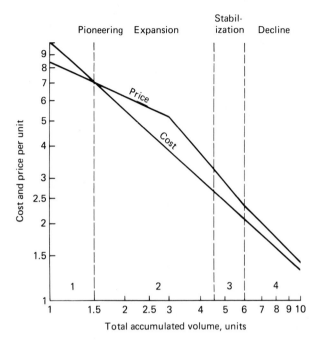

Figure 11-4 Price and cost patterns.

Price and Market Share

Figure 11-4 shows four stages of price/cost patterns.[4] While these patterns are being discussed, note the similarities between them and the product life cycle that was discussed in Chapter 2. Stage 1 of the price/cost pattern is an effort by firms to introduce the new product on the market, and they sell it below cost. This stage is similar to the pioneering phase of development of the product life cycle. Stage 2 of the price/cost pattern is similar to the expansion phase of the product life cycle. This stage is characterized by increasing competition because other firms recognize opportunities for profit and enter the industry. Consequently, the dominant producer may lose some of its market share. Thus an important strategy is to gain maximum market share as soon as possible, enter new markets, and differentiate products. During this stage, profits rise as the total dollar volume of sales increases. As shown in Figure 11-4, costs decline at a more rapid rate than prices as the industry gains "experience." During the latter part of this stage, some excess productive capacity may appear in the industry. Moreover, sales are growing, but at a slower pace. The time has come for a "shakeout"—stage 3. One of the producers may cut price in an effort to increase its market share. The weaker firms, those with high costs and small market shares,

---

[4]Both output and prices are expressed in current terms. Thus prices must be deflated to adjust for inflation.

will not survive. This is the time when firms try to maintain or expand market share, enter new markets, and diversify. The final stage of the price/cost pattern is when cost and price stability return. During this stage, the cost continues to decline as industry output increases. However, the "margin" between price and cost has narrowed substantially. Obviously cost and price will decline only to a level where they are "reasonable." By now the market shares of the various firms are well established and the profits are no longer high enough to attract many new entrants into the industry. During this declining phase, firms cut costs and phase out the unprofitable products.

The duration of the stages will vary from industry to industry. Note that the stages are discussed in terms of accumulated experience rather than time. The question of time is discussed next.

Strategic Implications

It is a fundamental rule of nature that the fittest of a species survives. In this case, the fittest firms are those with large market shares and the weakest are those with small market shares. Therefore, a producer should strive to obtain a dominant share of a *growing* market. If the market is stagnant or declining, perhaps strategy would be to get out of it.

The rate of growth of the market is very important. If the physical growth rate of output is 4 percent, the output will double in about 24 years. However, if the physical growth rate of output is 10 percent, the output will double in about 7 years. If the growth rate is 26 percent, it takes only about 3 years to double the output.[5]

In addition to the growth rate, one has to consider the rate of price declines (slope of the experience curves) each time the output doubles. For example, if the growth rate of output is 4 percent and there is no price decline, the output will, as previously noted, double in 24 years. However, if the price declines 20 percent (an 80 percent experience curve) each time output doubles, and the growth rate of output is 4 percent, the time required for the physical output to double will be reduced to 16 years. Similarly, if the growth rate is 10 percent and the price decline is 20 percent each time output doubles, the time required to double the output is 5 years.

Here are some of the strategic implications of market growth and experience curves.

1 Producers in industries that are growing rapidly and have large price declines every time physical output doubles will have to take into account the large capital investments that are required for production and to maintain or

---

[5]The time required to double the output can be determined for any growth rate by dividing that rate into 72. For example, if the growth rate were 15 percent, the time required to double the output would be 72/15 = 4.8 years. See Chapter 7 for additional information.

gain market share. Otherwise, they may be committed to invest more than they can afford to maintain market share.

2 A large market share can be attained in a very short period of time in industries that are growing rapidly and have large price declines. If a new producer with zero share of the market could capture 50 percent of the growth, that producer would have about 25 percent of the entire market in the 4 or 5 years required to double the physical output.

3 The costs per unit will probably decline the fastest for those producers who are gaining the largest market shares. Such producers are in a strong position to gain additional shares of the market by cutting price to discourage competition, innovating new products or methods of distributions, or segmenting the market.

PORTFOLIO STRATEGY[6]

This section demonstrates how to use information about market share and market growth to make strategic decisions about the growth potential of individual firms, divisions, or products. The basic tool that is used throughout this section is a matrix such as the one shown in Figure 11-5. The two vertical columns of the matrix designate high or low market shares for individual producers. The two rows of the matrix designate high or low growth rates for particular industries or markets. The strategies that are developed here may be used in conjunction with the market strategies explained earlier in the chapter. However, matrices shown in Figures 11-1 and 11-5 are substantially different in content, although both contain two rows (horizontal) and two columns (vertical).

Growth Potential for the Individual Producer

The first quadrant in Figure 11-5 shows that the individual producer has a low market share in an industry that has a high rate of growth. This position is typical of many companies that are introducing a new product. The earnings from that product are relatively low and the producer will be a net user of cash.

---

[6]Portfolio strategies should not be confused with portfolio theory, which is explained in Chapter 12. Portfolio strategy is the generally accepted term for the methods described in this chapter. For additional information about portfolio strategy, refer to the following sources:

Derek F. Abell and John S. Hammond, *Strategic Market Planning, Problems and Analytical Approaches.* Englewood Cliffs, N.J.: Prentice-Hall, Inc., 1979, chap. 4.

E. F. Dourlet, "Growth through Corporate Marketing Planning," *Planning for Corporate Growth*, Surendra Singhvi and Subhash C. Jain, eds. Oxford, Ohio: Planning Executives Institute, 1974, pp. 85–93.

Richard Lickridge, V. P. Norton Simon Corp. A presentation at "Managing a Diversified Company" sponsored by the Financial Analysts Federation, New York, Mar. 10, 1976.

J. W. McSwiney, "Route to Corporate Growth," *Planning for Corporate Growth*, ibid., pp. 13–22.

Frank T. Paine and William Naumes, *Strategy and Policy Formation: An Integrative Approach.* Philadelphia, Pa.: W. B. Saunders Company, 1974, pp. 157–161.

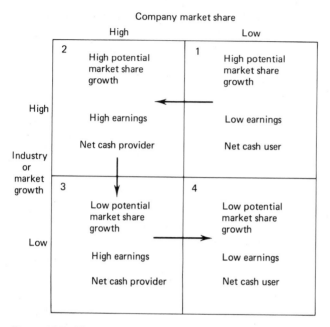

Figure 11-5 Market-share potential.

This means that the producer will require funding in order to support the operations necessary to produce and market the product. The term "funding" is used here in the general sense of the word. It means all the financial resources at the disposal of management. More will be said about the financial implications of the strategies shortly.

If the producer is successful, it will gain a high market share and move into the second quadrant. As one would expect, the earnings are high, but the firm still requires substantial funding to support its growth. Eventually, the rate of growth of the industry slows and the producer moves into the third quadrant. In quadrant 3, the producer still has a large share of the market and the earnings remain at a high level. However, now the producer does not have to finance "growth" because the growth rate of the industry has declined. Therefore, it has surplus funds that can be used elsewhere in the company. If the producer loses market share when the industry growth rate is declining (quadrant 4), the earnings will be reduced and it will become a net user of cash to maintain its low market share.

Diversified Firms

The same conceptual framework can be used to examine the portfolios of firms that have several divisions or products. Figure 11-6 shows the same four quadrants that were shown in Figure 11-5, but they are labeled differently. The first quadrant is labeled *opportunities* because of the potential that exists for a firm or division to capture a large share of a rapidly growing market. The second quadrant is labeled *stars* because these are the best performers. They have a large market share in a rapidly growing market and are making high returns. The third quadrant is labeled *cash cows* because firms or divisions in this quadrant can supply funds to those in quadrants 1 and 2. The fourth quadrant is called *dogs* as used in the derogatory sense of the word. These are the worst performers, and there is little chance for improvement. The circles represent individual products, divisions, or companies, and the diameters of the circles represent the annual volume of output, sales, or asset size.

Viewing a company in a portfolio context provides unique insights. For example, assume that the circles shown in Figure 11-6 represent the annual sales volume of the various divisions of a diversified company. By examining the growth potential of each of the divisions in this manner, the company may decide to divest itself of the dog and use the cash cow to support the growth of stars and other investment opportunities. Another insight concerns the allocation of capital. As a general matter, capital is allocated on the basis of the rate of return, and little consideration is given to growth potential of the investment. It is possible that some projects that are dogs may have a higher return than some projects that are investment opportunities. Therefore, a firm may allocate funds to the dogs instead of the opportunities. By viewing all projects in a portfolio context, funds can be channeled into those projects that offer the highest

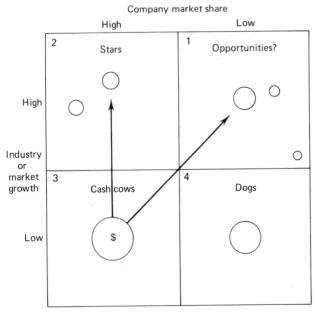

O = product, division, company
Diameter of O - annual volume or asset size

Figure 11-6 Strategic mix.

returns consistent with the general strategy of the business. The matrix also can be used to chart the development of a company, division, or product. The course of development should flow from quadrant 1 to quadrants 2, 3, and 4. However, many companies start at quadrant 2, and then go backward to quadrants 1 and 4. Needless to say, the former path to growth is preferred to the latter, which is designed to produce tax losses.

The matrices in Figures 11-5 and 11-6 provide additional perspectives on the life cycle. As shown in Figure 11-7, the four portfolio categories are superimposed on the life cycle. Thus the stars exist during the later portion of the expansion phase and opportunities during the later portion of the expansion phase. Cash cows are associated with stabilization, and dogs are associated with the declining phase.

It may also be useful to reconsider the key financial variables associated with each phase of the cycle and portfolio category. These variables were explained in the previous chapter. As shown in Figure 11-7, the stars have a high degree of leverage and pay small cash dividends—if any at all—in order to accelerate their growth. In contrast, the cash cows are reducing their leverage and increasing their cash dividends. Thus Figure 11-7 provides a visual integration of selected portfolio and financial strategies.

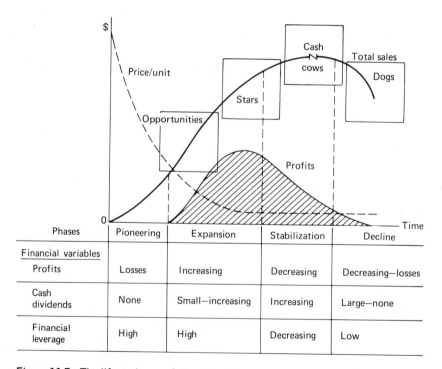

Phases	Pioneering	Expansion	Stabilization	Decline
Financial variables				
Profits	Losses	Increasing	Decreasing	Decreasing—losses
Cash dividends	None	Small—increasing	Increasing	Large—none
Financial leverage	High	High	Decreasing	Low

Figure 11-7 The life cycle, portfolio categories, and financial variables.

A Look at Competition

The matrix can also be used to examine the market shares and growth potential of competing firms. Figures 11-8 and 11-9 show two variants of the matrix. Figure 11-8 shows the "relative market share," which is plotted on a logarithmic scale. The word "relative" is used in at least two ways. The first usage is relative to the *largest producer*. Thus a business that is positioned at 2 on the log scale has twice the market share of the next largest producer, whereas a business positioned at 0.5 has one-half the market share of the largest producer. The second use of the term is relative to the *average size* of all producers. Using this measure, a business positioned at 2 would be twice as large as the average firm, and one positioned at 0.5 would be half as large as the average firm. Both methods give a "relative"measure and show approximately the same results.

Assume that the circles shown in Figure 11-8 represent all the firms in a given industry and that the diameter of the circles indicates their annual sales volume. The competitive picture is that the majority of companies in that industry are dogs or cash cows (quadrants 4 and 3). There are only two stars and one opportunity (quadrants 2 and 1), both of which are relatively small. Therefore, if a new company wanted to enter the industry by merger, the logical candidate would be one of two small stars or the one opportunity. By looking

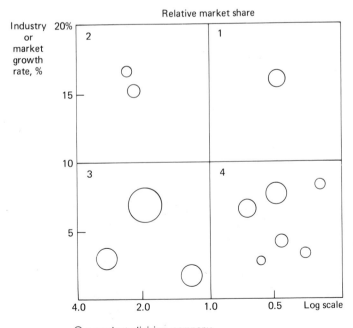

O = product, division, company
Diameter of O = annual volume or asset size

Figure 11-8 A look at competition.

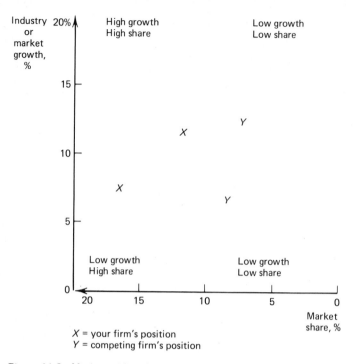

Figure 11-9   Market grid analysis.

at the industry in terms of market share and growth, the company wanting to enter the industry by merger avoided the possibility of acquiring one of the dogs because the price was "cheap."

Figure 11-9 shows an alternative method of plotting the market share. In this figure, each firm's percentage share of the market is plotted instead of the "relative" market share.

Table 11-1   Comparison of Methods

Producers	Output	Relative market share[†]	Percent of market	Growth rate, %
1	1000	1.54	19.2	4
2	300	0.46	5.8	15
3	400	0.62	7.7	5
4	500	0.77	9.6	12
5	600	0.92	11.5	2
6	700	1.08	13.5	12
7	800	1.23	15.4	18
8	900	1.38	17.3	8
Total output	5200		100.0	
Average output	650			

[†]Relative to average output.

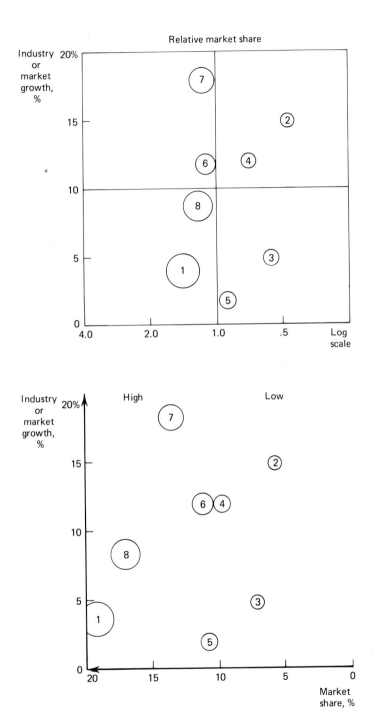

Figure 11-10 Comparison of methods.

Both methods give the same picture, but from a different perspective. By way of illustration, consider the data presented in Table 11-1 and the graphical representation of those data in Figure 11-10. Each circle represents a producer that is designated by number. The size of the circle is based on the output of each producer. Therefore, producer 1 has the largest circle and producer 2 the smallest circle. The top panel of the figure shows the market share relative to the size of the average producer (650). The bottom panel shows the market share expressed as percent of total market. The point is that both methods reveal about the same information and the user has to decide which of the two methods is appropriate.

CONCLUSION

This chapter examined market strategies, experience curves, and portfolio strategies. The first market strategy is to gain a larger share of the existing market. The second is to differentiate the product. The third is to present new products in new markets, and the fourth is diversification. The first strategy ties in most closely with the next two topics, experience curves and portfolio strategies. The concept of experience curves is that per-unit costs decline by a more or less constant percentage as industry output (experience) increases. Firms that produce the largest outputs tend to have the lowest costs and to be the most profitable. Thus some firms have strategies aimed at managing their costs in an attempt to gain market share. Mead Corporation is one such company, and its strategies are examined in Chapter 13. The section on portfolio strategy demonstrated how to use information about industry growth and market share to evaluate the growth potential of individual firms, divisions, or products. Firms are classified according to their growth potential, which reflects their relative position on the life cycle. Firms that are in the expansion phase of the life cycle are called stars, and those in the declining phase are dogs. By considering firms in the context of the life cycle or the portfolio strategy, managers may gain useful insights in developing profitable strategies.

QUESTIONS[†]

1 Referring to Figure 11-1, which of the market strategies shown is the most risky? Which is the least risky?
2 What is the significance of the 75 percent learning curve?
3 Why is having the lowest cost important?
4 What should be the financial strategies of a firm that is a "star"?
5 List three advantages of using portfolio strategy.

[†]Selected Solutions at end of book.

BIBLIOGRAPHY

Abell, Derek F., and John S. Hammond. *Strategic Market Planning, Problems and Analytical Approaches.* Englewood Cliffs, N.J.: Prentice-Hall, Inc., 1979.

Jain, Subhash, and Surendra Singhvi, eds. *Essentials of Corporate Planning.* Oxford, Ohio: Planning Executives Institute, 1973.

Perspectives on Experience. Boston, Mass.: The Boston Consulting Group, Inc., 1972.

Singhvi, Surendra, and Subhash Jain, eds. *Planning for Corporate Growth.* Oxford, Ohio: Planning Executives Institute, 1974.

Steiner, George A. *Strategic Managerial Planning.* Oxford, Ohio: Planning Executives Institute, 1977.

Chapter 12

Risk and Returns
  Expected Returns
  Risk
  Systematic Risk
  Unsystematic Risk
  Diversification

Portfolio Selection
  Dominance Rules
  Efficient Portfolio
  Portfolio Theory, Portfolio Strategy, and the Life Cycle

Capital Market Line (CML)

Conclusion

Questions

Bibliography

Portfolio Theory: A Planning Tool

Portfolio theory deals with the rules for the intelligent selection of assets under conditions of risk. Do not confuse portfolio theory with the portfolio strategies that were presented in the previous chapter. They are distinctly different concepts with similar names. Much of the research concerning portfolio theory has been directed toward the securities markets. Consequently, some of the terminology is investment-oriented. Nevertheless, some concepts developed in portfolio theory can be applied to strategic planning. By way of illustration, consider the case of Applied Technologies, a large diversified manufacturing company. Applied Technologies has grown rapidly in recent years and is currently evaluating its eight operating divisions. As part of the introspection process, the growth potential of each division was analyzed in terms of its current position on the life cycle. For convenience, the eight divisions are denoted by the letters A through H, and their positions on the life cycle are depicted in Figure 12-1. The company is going to use portfolio theory to provide information about which divisions should be retained, which should be sold, and new companies that may be acquired. This chapter explains some of the major features of portfolio theory and applies them to the Applied Technologies strategic plan.

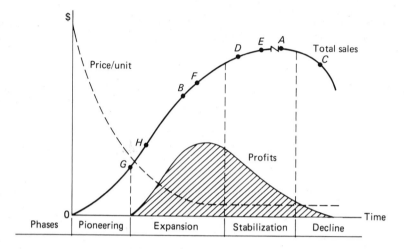

Figure 12-1 The life cycle and Applied Technologies' Divisions A to H.

RISK AND RETURNS

Portfolio theory deals with the rules for the selection of assets under conditions of risk. It is generally recognized that there is a trade-off between risk and return. The trade-off for investors who are averse to risk is depicted in Figure 12-2. The line representing the trade-off increases gradually as risk increases and then

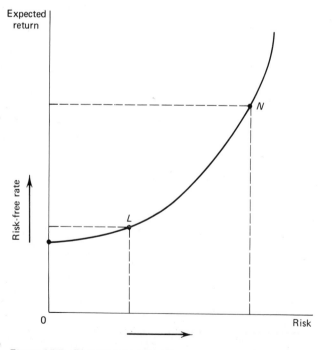

Figure 12-2 Risk-return trade-off.

becomes almost vertical at high levels of risk. This pattern indicates that investors will take on additional risk only if it is accompanied by additional returns. It also indicates that there are limits to the amount of risk that investors are willing to take, no matter what level of return is expected. Points L and N on the trade-off line represent investments in two assets. Point L has relatively low risk and a low expected return. Point N has a high degree of risk and a commensurately higher expected return. The terms " expected return" and "risk" have a particular meaning in portfolio theory. The process of portfolio selection will be explained after these terms have been defined.

Expected Returns

Before Applied Technologies acquires a new company, it calculates the expected returns that can be earned on that investment. The company also calculates the expected returns for its operating divisions during the introspection phase of its planning process. The *expected return* is the most likely return; it is defined as the sum of the products of the possible return times the probabilities. The calculations for the expected return for Division H are shown in Table 12-1. The first column lists some of the possible returns that are based on management estimates. Management also estimated the probability of occurrence for each of the returns listed in the first column. The probability of earning 5 percent is 20 percent. In other words, the chances are 20 out of 100 that Division H will earn 5 percent. Similarly, the chances are 17.5 out of 100 that Division H will earn 20 percent. When all the probabilities are summed, they must equal 1 or 100 percent. Next, the possible returns are multiplied by the probabilities and summed. The result is the expected return, which in this case is 10 percent. Stated otherwise, 10 percent is the most likely return that Division H can expect to earn.

Risk

Although Division H is *expected* to earn 10 percent, it may earn more or less than that amount. The terms *risk* or *total risk* refer to the extent to which the

Table 12-1   Expected Return *Er* for Division H

Possible returns r_t	Probability of outcomes p_t	$r_t p_t$
0.00	0.175	0.000
0.05	0.200	0.010
0.10	0.250	0.025
0.15	0.200	0.030
0.20	0.175	0.035
	1.00	Expected return = 0.100

$$Er = \sum_{t}^{n} p_t r_t = 0.100 = 10 \text{ percent}$$

Table 12-2 Standard Measure of Risk for Division H

Possible returns r_i	Expected return Er	Deviation from Er_i	(Deviation)^2 d_i^2	Probability of outcome p_i	(Deviation)^2 × probability
0.00	0.10	0.10	0.0100	0.175	0.00175
0.05	0.10	0.05	0.0025	0.200	0.00050
0.10	0.10	0.00	0.0000	0.250	0.00000
0.15	0.10	−0.05	0.0025	0.200	0.00050
0.20	0.10	−0.10	0.0100	0.175	0.00175

$$\text{Variance } \sigma^2 = 0.00450$$
$$\text{Standard deviation } \sigma = \sqrt{\sigma^2}$$
$$\sigma = \sqrt{0.00450}$$
$$= 0.0670 = 6.7\% \cong$$
$$7 \text{ percentage}$$
$$\text{points}$$

$$\text{Standard deviation } \sigma = \sqrt{\sum_i^n p_i[r_i - Er_i]^2}$$

returns may vary from the expected return. A proxy for total risk may be measured in statistical terms by the standard deviation of the expected return. *Standard deviation*, designated by the Greek letter sigma (σ), is a statistical technique that measures the variability of a set of observations from the average or predicted value of a distribution. The calculation of the standard deviation of the expected return for Division H is presented in Table 12-2. The sum of the values in the right-hand column is called the variance. The square root of the

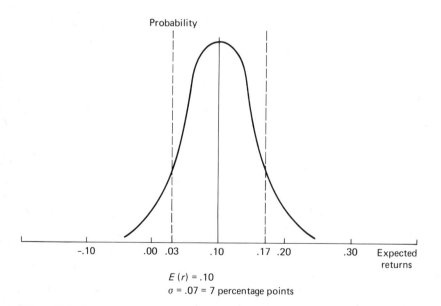

$E(r) = .10$

$\sigma = .07 = 7$ percentage points

Figure 12-3 Possible returns for Division H.

variance is the standard deviation, which is 0.0670, or approximately 7 percentage points rate of return.

If the probability distribution of the expected returns is normal or symmetric, as shown in Figure 12-3, one standard deviation includes about 34 percent of the area under the curve to the left of the expected return (0.10) and 34 percent of the area under the curve to the right of the expected return. This means that the chances are about 68 (34 percent + 34 percent = 68 percent) out of 100 that actual returns from Division H will be between 3 percent (0.10 − 0.07 = 0.03) and 17 percent (0.10 + 0.07 = 0.17). If the standard deviation had been say 15 percent, the chances would have been 68 out of 100 that the actual returns would fall between − 0.05 percent (0.10 − 0.15 = − 0.05) and 25 percent. A large standard deviation implies more risk than a small one.

Systematic Risk

Total risk can be divided into two categories, systematic and unsystematic risk. *Systematic risk* is risk that is attributable to a common source such as changing economic, social, or political conditions, and it affects the rate of return for all assets in the same manner. The degree of systematic risk can be measured by *beta*, which is an index of how the return of one asset tends to vary with changes in the returns for all assets.[1] The concept of beta was introduced in Chapter 2 in connection with the risk associated with different phases of the life cycle. A beta of 1 suggests that the return of an asset tends to be the same as for the market as a whole. A beta of 1.60 suggests that the returns of an asset tend to vary 60 percent more (in either direction) than the returns of the market as a whole. For example, as noted in Chapter 2, National Semiconductor common stock had a beta of 1.70, McDonald's had a beta of 1.50, and Safeway had a beta of 0.93.

Systematic risk cannot be eliminated by diversification because all assets are affected by it in the same manner. However, the average systematic risk of a portfolio of assets can be changed by altering the proportion of high-risk and low-risk assets that are held. Consider, for example, all the divisions of Applied Technologies as one portfolio, each division having the betas listed in Table 12-3. The third column in Table 12-3 lists the proportion of the total portfolio accounted for by each division. For example, Division A accounts for 15 percent of the total portfolio and has a beta of 0.9. Division F accounts for 5 percent of the total portfolio and has a beta of 1.2. When the betas for each division are multiplied by their respective proportions and summed, the result is the average

---

[1] Beta is defined as

$$Er_{it} - r_{ft} = b_i (Er_{mt} - r_{ft})$$

where Er_{it} = expected return on asset i in period t
$\quad r_{ft}$ = riskless rate in period t
$\quad Er_{mt}$ = expected return on portfolio in period t
b_i or beta = systematic risk measure of asset i relative to the portfolio

Table 12-3 Average Portfolio Beta

Division (1)	Beta (2)	Proportion of total portfolio (3)	(2) × (3) (4)	Revised proportions* (5)	(2) × (5) (6)
A	0.9	0.15	0.135	0.20*	0.180
B	1.3	0.05	0.065	0.05	0.065
C	0.6	0.35	0.210	0.00*	0.000
D	1.1	0.20	0.220	0.20	0.220
E	0.9	0.05	0.045	0.05	0.045
F	1.2	0.05	0.060	0.05	0.060
G	1.5	0.05	0.075	0.20*	0.300
H	1.3	0.10	0.130	0.25*	0.260
		100%	0.940 Average portfolio beta	100%	1.13 Average portfolio beta

portfolio beta. The average portfolio beta of 0.940 means that the returns of Applied Technologies tend to vary about 94 percent as much as the returns for the stock market as a whole. In other words, if the returns on the stock market increase 10 percent, the returns of Applied Technologies can be expected to increase 9.4 percent on average.

As part of the planning process, the management of Applied Technologies examines a number of alternative scenarios concerning the redistribution of their assets and risk. One scenario is to sell Division C and increase the investments in Divisions A, G, and H. The revised proportions of the total portfolio are denoted by an asterisk * in column 5 of Table 12-3. When the revised proportions are multiplied by the division betas, the average portfolio beta for Applied Technologies increases to 1.13. This example demonstrates that the systematic risk of a portfolio can be changed by altering the proportions of the assets in that portfolio.

Unsystematic Risk

Unsystematic risk can be eliminated by diversification. *Unsystematic risk* is risk that is attributable to unique events such as a fire, flood, strike, or the loss of a key employee, which affect the returns of a particular company. Such risk can be eliminated by proper diversification because the effect of a fire or flood on the returns of one company should have no relationship to the returns of other companies. A recent study of diversification has shown that unsystematic risk can be virtually eliminated by investing in as few as 11 different companies.[2] As

[2]J. H. Evans and S. H. Archer, "Diversification and the Reduction of Dispersion: An Imperial Analysis," *The Journal of Finance*, December 1968, pp. 761–767.

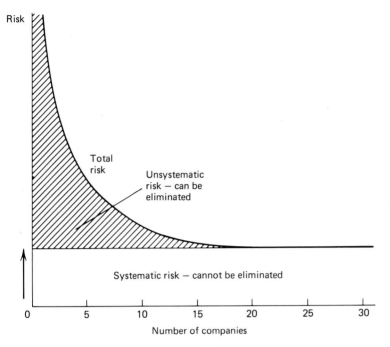

Figure 12-4 Portfolio risk.

shown in Figure 12-4, investing in a larger number of companies does not further reduce the level of risk in the portfolio.

Diversification

Another aspect of risk concerns the relationship between the returns for all the
divisions of the company or all the assets in the portfolio. The *principle of*

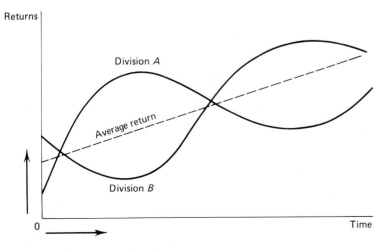

Figure 12-5 Principle of diversification.

diversification is to eliminate unsystematic risk and invest in assets whose variations in returns tend to offset each other. As shown in Figure 12-5, the returns for Division A and Division B offset each other, so that when they are combined, the joint return is less variable than the returns from either division. An additional example may be helpful. A portfolio consisting of General Motors, Ford, Chrysler, and American Motors would be riskier than one consisting of General Motors, Xerox, Chase Manhattan Bank, and Procter & Gamble. This is so because the first portfolio consists exclusively of automotive companies. A common factor such as a shortage of gasoline affects the returns of all the automotive companies in the same manner. In contrast, a shortage of gasoline will not have the same impact on Xerox, Chase Manhattan Bank, or Procter & Gamble. Consequently, the average portfolio risk has been reduced by investing in companies whose returns are not affected by the same factors.

PORTFOLIO SELECTION

After the risks associated with individual assets have been recognized, the task remains of selecting those assets that provide the best combinations of risk and return.

Dominance Rules

The assets that provide the best relationship between risk and return are selected on the basis of two dominance rules.

Rule 1 Assets with the *least risk* are preferred to all other assets with the same rate of return.

Rule 2 Assets with the *highest expected returns* are preferred to all other assets with the same degree of risk.

The eight divisions of Applied Technologies are used to illustrate the dominance rules. Each division is considered a separate asset. To ease explanation,

Table 12-4 Expected Returns and Risk for Applied Technologies' Eight Divisions

Division	Expected returns, %	Risk σ, %
A	5	2
B	8	12
C	4	2
D	8	4
E	6	8
F	7	11
G	11	11
H	10	7

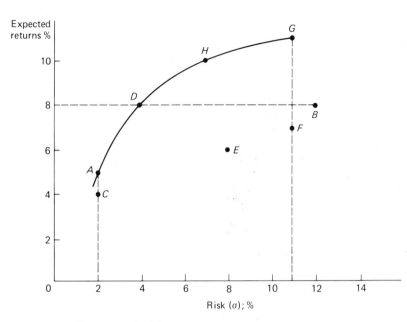

Figure 12-6 Eight assets in risk-return space.

the data presented in Table 12-4 are also depicted in Figure 12-6. On the basis of the first rule, Division A dominates Division B. Divisions D and B have the same expected return (8 percent), but Division D is less risky than Division B (σ_D = 4 percent, σ_B = 12 percent). On the basis of the second rule, Division G dominates Division F. Both divisions have the same degree of risk (σ = 11 percent), but Division G has a higher expected return than Division F (11 percent vs. 7 percent). Division A dominates Division C for the same reason. Thus Divisions C, E, F, and B are inferior to the other divisions that have higher expected returns and less risk.

Efficient Portfolio

An *efficient portfolio* consists of dominant assets. As shown in Figure 12-6, Divisions A, D, H, and G are the dominant divisions. The line ADHG is called an efficient frontier. It is the locus of points that offers the maximum rate of return for each degree of risk in the set of assets that are under consideration.

Portfolio Theory, Portfolio Strategy, and the Life Cycle

Applied Technologies combined the information obtained from analyzing the dominant divisions with information about the life cycle and portfolio strategies in graphic form (Figure 12-7). Based on the combined analysis, Applied Technologies decided to retain Divisions G, H, B, F, D, and A and sell Divisions E and C. Although Division C accounts for 35 percent of the total portfolio of Applied Technologies, it is a *dog*, and the outlook for that division is not good. Division E is a *cash cow* and accounts for only 5 percent of the total portfolio. The

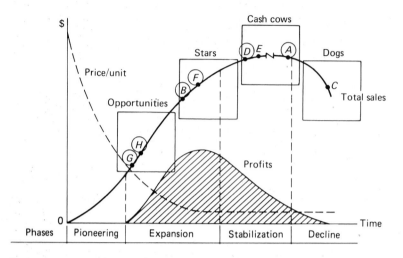

Figure 12-7   The life cycle, Applied Technologies' Divisions A to H, portfolio categories.

returns of this division are too low relative to its risk. Therefore, Applied Technologies sold the two divisions and reallocated the funds among divisions with better prospects for growth. The divisions that were retained have a circle drawn around them to make their location on the life cycle stand out. The figure shows that the company is retaining the cash cows (Divisions D and H) to provide funds for the stars (Divisions B and F) and the opportunities (Divisions G and F). Applied Technologies also uses this combination of techniques for screening hundreds of potential acquisition candidates.

CAPITAL MARKET LINE (CML)

The previous section focused on risky assets such as the various divisions of Applied Technologies. Now the analysis is extended to include risk-free assets. In order to do this, it is necessary to develop the capital market line (CML) that is depicted in Figure 12-8. The return on the risk-free asset is represented by point R_f, which is located on the vertical axis. U.S. Treasury securities can be thought of as being assets that are free of risk. Such assets have relatively low returns and no risk ($\sigma = 0$). Point M represents a market portfolio of risky assets that is recognized by all investors as being the best combination of risk and return. It is the optimum combination of risky assets. In theory, the return on the market portfolio E_M is the weighted average return on all assets in the market. In practice, it is analogous to the return on Standard and Poor's 500 stock index or some similar stock-market indicator.

   Various combinations of *efficient portfolios* consisting of combinations of risk-free and risky assets can be constructed on the capital market line. This means that the portfolios contain only *systematic risk*, except those with a risk-

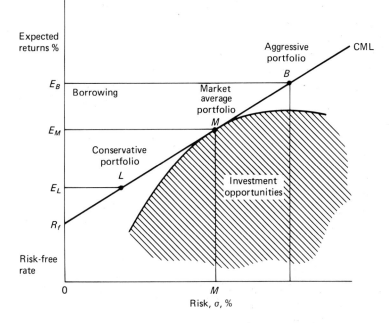

Figure 12-8 Capital market line (CML).

free return R_f where $\sigma = 0$. In other words, the portfolios are efficiently diversified because all the unsystematic risk has been removed.

Against this background, funds can be invested in the following manner:

- All funds can be invested in a risk-free asset that will yield a low rate of return R_f.
- All funds can be invested in the market portfolio M, which will provide an expected return of E_M, which is higher than the return on the risk-free asset.
- Some of the funds can be invested in the risk-free asset and the remainder in the market portfolio. Point L represents such a combination portfolio and has an expected return of R_L, which is lower than the expected return on the market portfolio and higher than the risk-free return.
- Assume that funds can be borrowed at the risk-free rate and invested in the market portfolio M. Point B represents portfolios in which borrowed funds were used to increase the size of the investment in the market portfolio. The borrowing increased both the risk and the expected return E_B.

Points L, M, and B can be considered in a slightly different context. Point L can be considered "conservative" because of the proportion of funds invested in risk-free assets. For example, if Applied Technologies was considered a "conservative" firm, it might keep a significant portion of its total assets invested in short-term marketable securities. Point M is the "market average" portfolio. In this case, the risk and returns will be about the same as the risk and returns on say the Standard and Poor's 500 stock average. Point *M* is an "aggressive" portfolio. In this case, Applied Technologies is willing to borrow in order to increase their total investment in the market portfolio of assets. Stated otherwise, the firm wants a higher rate of return and is willing to take on the higher degree of risk that is necessary to obtain it.

CONCLUSION

Portfolio theory is a planning tool that provides greater understanding of diversification and asset selection under conditions of risk. The terms risk and return have special meanings in portfolio theory. Risk refers to the variability of expected returns. Moreover, total risk consists of systematic and unsystematic risk. Systematic risk is common to all assets and cannot be removed by diversification. However, the level of systematic risk in a portfolio of assets can be changed by altering the proportions of the assets in that portfolio. Unsystematic risk is risk that is unique and can be eliminated by diversification. The principle of diversification is to eliminate unsystematic risk and invest in assets whose variations in returns tend to offset each other. Next, the selection of efficient portfolio consists of selecting those risky assets that give the best combinations of risk and return. The risks and returns can be modified by investing in risk-free assets or by borrowing funds and increasing both the risk and expected returns.

Applied Technologies used portfolio theory in conjunction with the life cycle and portfolio strategies to make strategic decisions with respect to the operating divisions that should be retained or sold.

QUESTIONS[†]

1 Explain the meaning of the terms *risk* and *return*.
2 What is beta?
3 Does the fact that a company has many different assets mean that it is efficiently diversified? Justify your answer.
4 Discuss the financial strategies that may be appropriate for Applied Technologies' Divisions G and A.
5 If you were making the decisions at Applied Technologies, would you favor portfolio *L*, *M*, or *B* in Figure 12-8? Explain your choice.

[†]Selected solutions at end of book.

BIBLIOGRAPHY

Bicksler, James L., ed. *Capital Market Equilibrium and Efficiency.* Lexington, Mass.: D. C. Heath and Company, 1977.

Francis, Jack Clark. *Investments: Analysis and Management*, 3d ed. New York: McGraw-Hill Book Company, 1980.

Francis, Jack Clark, and Stephen H. Archer. *Portfolio Analysis.* Englewood Cliffs, N.J.: Prentice-Hall, Inc., 1971.

Haley, Charles W., and Lawrence D. Schall. *The Theory of Financial Decisions.* New York: McGraw-Hill Book Company, 1973.

Markowitz, Harry M. *Portfolio Selection: Efficient Diversification of Investments.* New York: John Wiley & Sons, Inc., 1959.

Sharpe, William F. *Investments.* Englewood Cliffs, N.J.: Prentice-Hall, Inc., 1978.

———. *Portfolio Theory and Capital Markets.* New York: McGraw-Hill Book Company, 1970.

Smith, Keith V. *Portfolio Management.* New York: Holt, Rinehart and Winston, Inc., 1971.

Chapter 13

Strategic Planning at Mead: A Case Study

Mead is one of the nation's leading corporations and a leading advocate of strategic planning. This chapter is a case study of the development of strategic planning at Mead, as told by Warren L. Batts, who is Mead's president.[1] This case study is unique because it describes the evolution of strategic planning at a major corporation, their corporate goals, and some of the techniques that they used.

MEAD CORPORATION TODAY

Today, I'd like to discuss with you how one company, the Mead Corporation, views strategic planning. I am sure that the techniques and organization for a successful strategic planning system must vary with every company. I hope a case history of the evaluation of strategic planning in our company will provide you with helpful insights for your situation.

[1] Warren L. Batts, "Planning and the Corporation: What the Future Holds," A speech presented at *Business Week* Strategic Planning Conference, New York, Oct. 4, 1978. Reprinted by permission. Copyright The Mead Corporation.

To put my comments in perspective, let me briefly describe the company.

Mead is basically a forest products company. Nearly 80 percent of our earnings are derived from trees—from the manufacture of pulp, to the conversion of paperboard to beverage carriers, to distribution of school supplies.

We are also involved in energy—from the power we generate from wood, and other fuels to mining coal; to producing rubber products for the exploration and production of gas and oil; to the supplies we distribute to refineries, petrochemical and power plants, and to independent oil well drillers.

We are also developing technologies and new businesses for the future: primarily in storing, retrieving, and reproducing data.

In short, Mead is a company eager to grow in the industries in which it started, as well as to expand into industries which fit the capability and style of our management. For example, we are interested in certain chemical businesses on one hand—and on the other in the creation of entirely new businesses such as our computer-based legal research service known as Lexis.

We believe the vehicle for managing Mead today, and in the future, is our strategic-planning system.

CHANGES AT MEAD

From early 1973 to April of this year, I was the company's chief operating officer. With the other corporate officers, we helped our operating people through an extremely difficult period where we:

1 Shifted from centralized to decentralized management.

2 Shifted from making major capital decisions on a centralized basis, sometimes subjectively, in response to an emotional plea for capital—to a disciplined capital allocation process for funding strategies.

3 Changed the mind set of growing every business, just because we were in it, to achieving leadership or getting out.

In the process, we restructured our organization, changed managers, improved our management information systems, initiated special strategic studies to help particular business units, and focused everyone's attention on operating our businesses better.

ROLE OF STRATEGIC PLANNING AT MEAD

So let me try to define strategic planning in terms of what it means to us in Mead. First, it ensures that we're continually upgrading the quality of our organization and the professionalism of our managers by increasing our ability to put new techniques into practice and by expanding our competence and perspective as individuals. Next, it provides a discipline which helps us avoid the temptation to overstaff and overspend in good times and to slash costs hastily in downturns. Most important, when all is said and done, our process is primarily aimed at helping us achieve Mead's corporate objectives.

CORPORATE GOALS

In the late sixties, when we were beginning to develop our planning system, we quickly came to the question of what kind of company should Mead be. We decided, as an organization, that we wanted to be in the top quarter of those companies with whom we are normally compared—in other words, we wanted to be among the best in industry. We translated this objective into specific financial goals, given an average inflation rate of 6 percent:

1 We needed to achieve return on net assets of 12 percent; and
2 To maintain a debt/equity ratio of 50 percent
3 By achieving those results, we would attain a return on equity of 17 percent; and
4 A 10 percent sustainable growth rate.

These goals provided us with a sharper sense of direction than we'd had before, and they were definite milestones for measuring our progress.

DEVELOPING A STRATEGIC PLAN

At the time we were beginning to develop our strategic-planning approach, Mead was fairly diversified. We had 40 strategic business units. We needed rational methods to help us evaluate their strategies and make intelligent decisions in allocating our capital to fund those strategies.

To begin implementing this system, we conducted a series of seminars for our top 300 managers. We described the corporation's philosophy, the objectives we had set, and how we'd arrived at them. We presented the strategic-planning system as a tool, and made it clear that we expected our people to use it.

In 1972, we arrayed our businesses on a type of matrix (Figure 13-1) which is now familiar to most of you. We could see the growth rates of the market segments in which we were involved and what our competitive situations were in those markets. This kind of picture helped us to view graphically how Mead was balanced in terms of cash generation and cash use. Equally important, it enabled us to assess the growth potential of the total corporation.

It was a rigorous assessment, and the results were not comforting. It became clear we had several small business units in very weak competitive positions. Yet they were substantial users of cash which was needed elsewhere—in businesses where we had opportunities for significant growth.

Even though some of those high cash users were profitable, we chose to stick with our strategic criteria. We decided we wanted to look like this by 1977.

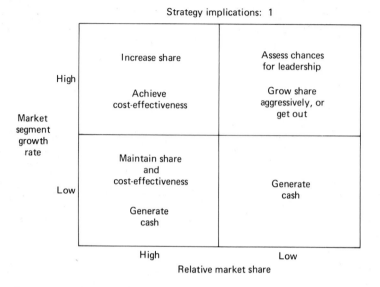

Figure 13-1 Strategy implications: 1—Relative market share.

Between 1973 and 1976, we disposed of 11 units which offered us neither growth nor significant cash flow. The $105 million we received for them was promptly reinvested in our stronger businesses, and as a result our mix of businesses showed substantial improvement by the end of 1976.

COST EFFECTIVENESS AND WORKING CAPITAL

During this period, we impressed our managers with the importance of cost effectiveness to our ability to compete in the marketplace. To us, the value of a large market share is the potential for lower costs than those of our competitors. As a consequence, a major portion of the $600 million we have invested in Mead and our affiliates since 1972 was aimed at increasing our cost effectiveness.

MARKET SHARE $\longrightarrow$ COST EFFECTIVENESS
$600 MILLION INVESTMENT

At the same time, we stressed better management of working capital and the fixed assets already in place. In 1972, our working capital per dollar of sales was almost 20 cents. By 1977, we had reduced working capital to 16 cents per dollar of sales. This accounted for a savings of $65 million in working capital in 1977. We intend to reduce this working capital to sales relationship even further in the years ahead.

With these changes, our results improved dramatically. Our sales have grown at a compound rate of 10 percent since 1972, in spite of our divestiture of businesses with sales of $180 million. By the end of 1977, our return on equity

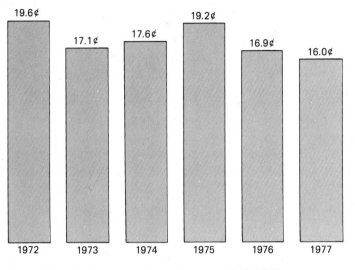

Figure 13-2 Working capital per sales dollar 1972–1977.

had reached 16 percent, very near our long-term goal of 17 percent. We had moved from twelfth to third place among the top forest-products companies, in terms of return on equity.

In other words, we have achieved our objective; we *are* in the upper quarter.

Furthermore, today we have clear plans for each of our businesses for the next 5 years. There will be exceptions, of course, as future events unfold, but we think we have a good idea of what Mead will be as a company in 1983.

To us, one of the most important aspects of the changes in Mead is how our people feel about our strategic-planning process. Today, our operating managers are very proud of the accomplishments of their business units. Each one believes that we could not have made the progress we have without our system. Each

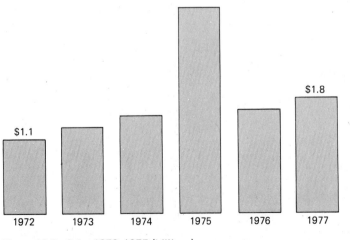

Figure 13-3 Sales 1972–1977 (billions).

believes it has evolved to be not just one of the best planning systems in our industry, but an important aspect of the "Mead culture."

EVOLUTION OF PLANNING

During this period, the role of planning has changed in Mead. It appears to me that there have been four distinct stages. First was the *preplanning stage*, the time when planning was largely the province of top management. That worked, so long as the company's range of market segments was fairly limited. It was a time when our management style was more centralized than it is today.

Table 13-1 Evolution of Planning at Mead: 1

1 Preplanning stage
 • Top-management-dominated
 • Limited portfolio
 • Centralized management

But by the late sixties, Mead was too large and too diverse for top management to run the company centrally and informally; so next came what I'll call the *initial stage* of our formal planning system. It started in the late sixties. Bill Wommack—now Mead's vice chairman—and a small planning staff not only defined the system but provided direct guidance to managers in applying it. The process at this stage tended to be numbers-oriented. We were trying to improve decisions by improving the underlying data.

Table 13-2 Evolution of Planning at Mead: 2

1 Preplanning stage
2 Initial stage—late sixties
 • Top-management-directed
 • Strong staff role
 • Numbers-oriented

We moved to the next phase around 1974 or 1975—I'll call it the *intermediate stage*. The basic system was in place by then, and the planning process began to focus increased attention on the issues rather than the numbers.

Table 13-3 Evolution of Planning at Mead: 3

1 Preplanning stage
2 Initial stage—late sixties
3 Intermediate stage—1974–1976
 • Issues-oriented
 • Top-management-committed
 • Active staff role

Top management at this stage was solidly committed to the planning system, but below the division level it was still perceived as being only marginally useful. Planning still required a lot of staff involvement. In other words, the system was working, but it had not yet become a way of life for most of our line managers.

Only in the last year or two have we begun to move into what we consider to be an *advanced stage*. Today:

1 Our managers do their own planning their own way within a set of general corporate guidelines.

2 Their commitment to their plans is much stronger. After all, *they* developed those plans.

3 To an increasing degree, our business plans determine the way decisions are made. There are fewer special cases or exceptions. I might add that one of our best measures of managers is their ability to determine what's in store for the business and build a plan that deals with that reality.

4 And more and more, performance is evaluated in terms of the quality of a plan, the manner in which it is executed, and the results achieved.

So, today the system *is* a way of life for most of our managers.

Now our planning approach is entering a new phase.

We are already using as sophisticated techniques as we can develop or find. We use experience curves, matrices, evaluator charts, computer modes, PIMS,[2] etc., and we will use other techniques as they arise. So the phase we're entering now has less to do with new techniques than with new purpose.

FUTURE DEMANDS ON THE PLANNING SYSTEM

Our planning must change in two major ways. First, it must become a more proactive stimulator of our business units. Until now, strategic planning at the corporate level has been a relatively passive, critiquing function. But the easy gains are behind us. Now it is essential for our line managers to be encouraged and aided in redefining our market segments, in order to uncover additional products and markets and to adapt our present production facilities to capitalize on those opportunities. Our short-term gains will most likely come from innovative product and process modifications and extensions.

Table 13-4 Future Demands on the Planning System

- More proactive
- Sharper focus
- Innovative
- Extended planning horizon
- Better risk analysis

[2]Acronym for Profit Impact of Market Strategy program of the Strategic Planning Institute.

This is a tall order. We can do it through more involvement of more people working to develop and to achieve more clearly defined goals.

The second change required is that we extend the range of our planning system beyond 5 years, to look ahead 10 to 20 years. The very nature of our businesses is such that most of our major capital projects are 20-year decisions. The cost of new facilities has soared until mistakes are large and unforgiving. Yet we must continue to grow in the eighties—in an environment vastly different from the sixties or even the seventies. In short, we must grow in a highly selective, highly focused manner—by looking far enough ahead to identify and truly understand the risks involved.

Table 13-5   Future Requirements of Planning at Mead

- Flexible enough for diverse strategies
- Improved measures of strategic performance
- Integration with human resources planning

In this delicate changing of our planning system, what it emphasizes will have an even more direct effect on the future course of our businesses than today. For example, if our system emphasizes the conservation of cash, our organization will tend to avoid risk taking. If it emphasizes only growth, our future will become far less stable. We believe some businesses should generate cash with little growth, some rapid growth requiring heavy investment. Therefore, our system must be flexible enough, with a positive approach, to value and encourage both kinds of businesses. In this way, we'll achieve overall balance.

This evaluation is going to require some corollary changes. For example, we must refine the ways in which we measure strategic expenditures—such as investments in new products—to keep them distinct from operating expenses. We cannot allow a project which requires, say, 7 years of steady funding to be whipsawed by the economic conditions of the moment.

People Are Important

Equally important, we believe it means that the selection, development, and compensation of people must be better linked to long-term business objectives.

For example, high reported earnings or cash flow is not expected from a new venture; rather, we need a manager able to solve problems and to gain market share quickly (see Figure 13-4). The worst kind of manager for such a business would be someone whose natural inclination is to be more concerned with cost control and net profit than with attracting other entrepreneurs and investing rapidly to build the business. That cost-control type of individual, however, would make an ideal manager of a very mature business in a low-growth market, since cash generation is the key for this type of business (see Figure 13-5). In other words, we must be more concerned with matching the right temperament with the right job.

Strategy implications: 2

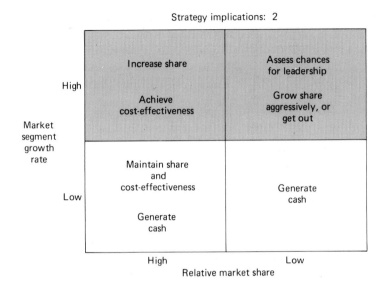

Figure 13-4 Strategy implications: 2—Relative market share.

Strategy implications: 3

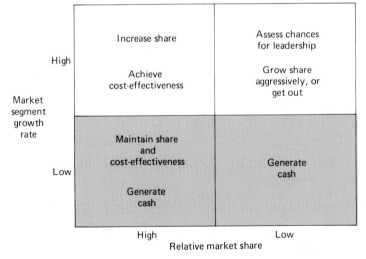

Figure 13-5 Strategy implications: 3—Relative market share.

FUTURE GOALS

In summary, we foresee four major needs that our planning system must meet in the future:

- It must be responsive enough to change with the development of our corporation. We've had success with the planning system we have today, and there will be reluctance to change it.

- Therefore, it must be continually updated and retaught. By that, I don't mean the preparation of forms or a manual. In fact, we are constantly on guard against overformalization which could lead to hardening of our arteries. Instead, we must provide the learning experiences which reduce our concepts to an intuitive level in each manager, and in the process, provide perspective and techniques that continue to broaden us as people.
- It must be inclusive enough to incorporate other disciplines, such as human resource planning, research and development, and long-range economic, political, and social analyses.
- Finally, it must be proactive enough to challenge the organization—to stimulate, to sharpen our ingenuity, and ultimately, to understand and to support operating managers as they take greater risks to generate new markets and new products for our future.

We believe our planning system will meet these needs. In the process, we believe the people in Mead will respond with greater motivation and stronger commitment—and a greater sense of personal achievement.

We have a philosophy at Mead that common needs and common beliefs bind people together.

We believe our strategic-planning process is a major ingredient in our particular "corporate environment." It is part of us, and we are each part of it. Through it, Mead will continue to advance among the top performers in American business.

QUESTIONS[†]

1 In what phase of the life cycle would you place the Mead Corporation?
2 In what phase of the life cycle would you place Lexis?
3 What is the role of strategic planning at Mead?
4 Approximately how many years did it take for Mead to evolve from the pre-planning stage to the advanced stage?
5 What is the role of people in strategic planning at Mead?

BIBLIOGRAPHY

Abell, Derek F., and John S. Hammond. *Strategic Market Planning, Problems and Analytical Approaches.* Englewood Cliffs, N.J.: Prentice-Hall, Inc., 1979.

Lorange, Peter, and Richard F. Vancil. *Strategic Planning Systems.* Englewood Cliffs, N.J.: Prentice-Hall, Inc., 1977.

Paine, Frank T., and William Naumes. *Strategy and Policy Formation: An Integrative Approach.* Philadelphia, Pa.: W. B. Saunders Company, 1974.

[†]Selected solutions at end of book.

Schollenbarger, Robert E. *Policy Formulation and Strategy Management.* New York: John Wiley & Sons, Inc., 1978.

Shirley, Robert C., Michael H. Peters, and Adel I. El-Ansary. *Strategy and Policy Formation: A Multifunctional Orientation.* New York: John Wiley & Sons, Inc., 1976.

Glossary

Acid-test ratio is a measure of liquidity and is derived by dividing cash, marketable securities, and net accounts receivable by current liabilities. It is a "narrow" measure of liquidity because it excludes inventories and prepaid items.

Annuity is a series of periodic payments that are usually made in equal amounts for a specified period of time.

Average collection period is a measure of efficiency that indicates the number of day's sales that are tied up in receivables. It is calculated by multiplying average accounts receivable by 360 days and dividing that amount by net sales.

Beta is an indicator of systematic risk. It is the slope b of a linear relationship between expected "excess" returns over a risk-free rate of individual stocks and the expected excess returns of a portfolio of stocks.

Break-even analysis is one of several methods that may be used to determine the economic feasibility of projects. It measures the amount of revenue needed to "break even" or cover all costs.

Capital Asset Pricing Model (CAPM) estimates the capitalization rate that is used in the dividend-valuation model.

Capitalization rate and discount rate are terms used interchangeably and refer to the interest rate used in the denominator of present-value equations.

Cash cow refers to a division that provides funds to other divisions within the same firm. The cash cow generates large sums that are needed by the growth divisions.

Compound interest is interest that is paid on the principal and interest earned in the previous periods of time.

Contingency plans are plans for occurrences that are not likely to occur. They shorten reaction time just in case the unlikely happens.

Cross selling means selling to *existing customers* a variety of services or products offered by the firm.

Debt coverage is calculated by dividing profit before interest and taxes by interest expense. It measures a company's ability to "cover" its fixed charges.

Declining phase of the product life cycle is the final phase of the life cycle. Sales decline and firms operate at a loss. Over time, firms will go out of business or be "rejuvenated" because the demand for their products has increased. This was the case of the coal industry, which was in the declining phase of the life cycle until higher energy prices made coal an attractive source of fuel.

Derived demand means the demand for one product that creates the demand for another. For example, the demand for automobiles creates the demand for tires.

Discount rate or capitalization rate are terms used interchangeably and refer to the interest rate used in the denominator of the present-value equations.

Diversification means to eliminate unsystematic risk by investing in assets whose variations in returns tend to offset each other.

Dividend-valuation model is one model that is used to determine the intrinsic value of common stock by discounting expected cash dividends by the appropriate rate.

Dominance rules are two rules in portfolio selection for selecting assets that provide the best risk-return relationships.

Earnings per share is calculated by dividing earnings available for common stockholders by the average number of shares outstanding.

Efficient frontier is the locus of points that offers the maximum rate of return for each degree of risk in the set of assets under consideration.

Elasticity of demand refers to the responsiveness of sales to a change in price.

Expansion phase of the product life cycle is the second phase of the product life cycle and is characterized by increased sales, rising profits, increasing competition, falling prices, and by some firms failing or being acquired by other business concerns.

Expected return is the most likely return, and it is defined as the sum of the products of the possible returns times their probabilities.

Experience curves are a concept used to calculate the reduction in unit cost every time total industry or firm output doubles.

External environment includes factors such as government control, new technology, and weather that are external to the firm but may influence its behavior.

Fixed-asset turnover indicates how efficiently fixed assets are being used and is calculated by dividing net sales by average total fixed assets.

Goals are specific targets or objectives such as a rate of return on assets of 15 percent.

Impact matrix is one of several techniques that may be used to determine threats or opportunities facing the firm.

Internal rate of return (IRR) is that rate of interest which equates the present value of cash flows to the investment outlay. It is a popular method used for ranking investment proposals.

Intrinsic value is the theoretical value of an asset and may not be the same as its market value.

Introspection means self-examination. It is the first step in the strategic-planning process and includes a management audit, an examination of the firm's financial condition, physical facilities, markets, and strategies.

Inventory turnover ratio measures how many times inventory is sold or turned over each year and is calculated by dividing cost of sales by average inventory.

Long-term debt as percent of total capital is one indicator of financial leverage that measures long-term debt expressed as a percent of total capital.

Market share refers to the percent of sales or assets for a determined number of firms that constitute a relevant market that is held by one or more firms. For example, Maurice Industries has 25 percent of the sales of the entire industry.

Mission is the corporate mission that tells what business a company is in. For example, Mobil is in the energy business.

Monte Carlo simulation is a simulation technique where the values of the variables are selected at random from a given set of parameters. It was used in the book to determine the intrinsic value of a firm.

Net present value is the present value of cash flows discounted at the cost of capital, and less the cost of the investment outlay. This is one of the most useful techniques that may be used to rank investment proposals.

Net working capital measures liquidity and is the difference between current assets and current liabilities.

Payback period is a technique used to measure the number of years required to return the net investment outlay of an investment proposal. This is a widely used method for making investment decisions.

Payout ratio is the cash dividends per share divided by the earnings per share. It is the proportion of earnings paid out in the form of cash dividends to holders of common stock.

Pioneering phase of product life cycle is the first phase of the life cycle and is characterized by the introduction of new products, a limited number of firms, losses, and high leverage.

Portfolio strategies is a method that uses market share and market growth to make strategic decisions about the growth potential of individual firms, divisions, or products. It is not the same as portfolio theory.

Portfolio theory deals with the intelligent selection of assets under conditions of risk. Do not confuse this with portfolio strategies.

Present value is one of the most important variants of the compound-interest equation. It indicates how much dollars received in the future will be worth today.

Product life cycle or life cycle refers to the four phases of development (pioneering, expansion, stabilization, and decline) that are experienced by products, companies, and organizations as they evolve over time.

Profit margin is a ratio of the net profit after taxes divided by net sales. It is the percent of profit earned for each dollar of sales.

Profitability index is the present value of cash flows discounted at the cost of capital, and divided by the investment outlay.

Rate of return on equity measures the return on owner's investment and is calculated by dividing net profits after taxes by average total stockholders' equity.

Reinvestment rate applies any time compound interest or one of its variants is used. It is the interest rate at which funds are reinvested.

Returns on total assets measures productivity and is calculated by dividing earnings before interest and taxes by average assets.

Risk refers to the variability of returns and may be measured by the standard deviation from the expected return. Total risk consists of systematic plus unsystematic risk.

Rule of 72 is the approximate length of time required for the principal amount to double in value when compounded at different rates of interest, and may be determined by dividing the interest rate into 72.

Scope of corporate operations tells where they are doing business and the product market. For example, Pizza Hut sells pizza and related products in the United States but is expanding to other countries.

Snowflake diagram is a graphic presentation that depicts the effort that is required to respond to particular threats or opportunities.

Stabilization phase of the product life cycle is the third phase of the product life cycle. During this phase, sales increase slowly while prices and profits decline. The number of firms continues to diminish.

Strategic planning and strategy are terms used here that refer to major action programs that are used by an organization to achieve its mission and goals.

Systematic risk is risk that is common to all securities and cannot be eliminated by diversification. It may be measured by beta.

Unsystematic risk is risk that is unique to one company or division and may be eliminated by efficient diversification.

Vulnerability analysis is a technique that may be used to determine how susceptible an organization is to threats or factors that may cause harm.

Selected Solutions

Chapter 1

1 Strategic planning refers to major action programs while budgeting is an accounting process. Budgeting is used to translate some aspects of the strategic plan into operational plans.

2 McDonald's is best known for its hamburgers and related products and Boeing for its aircraft. This, of course, does not answer the question, but it clarifies the companies involved.

3 Inflation
  Government regulations
  Taxes
  Increased participation in the labor force by women

5 The plans become less accurate as the time increases. Thus the plan for next year is expected to be reasonably accurate, but the plans for subsequent years become less accurate. Keep in mind that the future is a changing target. The likelihood of accurately predicting what the future will be 5 years from now is very small. The idea of planning is to track the elusive future continuously.

6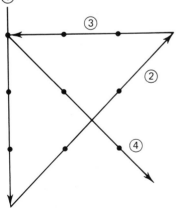

Chapter 2

1 The life cycle applies to all types of organizations.
3 Firms in the pioneering phase are heavy cash users. Because they are introducing new products, firms in this phase of the life cycle frequently experience financial losses.
4 Diversification and the addition of new products are two ways to extend the duration of the life cycle.
5 The most important strategy is to minimize costs. They should also consider selling the business or phasing it out before the diminishing profits turn into losses.

Chapter 3

1 Introspection means self-examination. It is the first step in the process of strategic planning. The idea is that a firm must know its existing strengths and weaknesses before it can make intelligent plans for the future.
2 The firm that is in the early expansion phase of the life cycle will probably have a high degree of financial leverage (this will be explained in Chapter 10), large cash requirements, increasing profits, and relatively small but increasing dividends. In the later stages of the stabilization phase of the life cycle, sales will increase at a modest pace; the firm will have less financial leverage and relatively large cash dividends, and it will be a net provider of cash funds.

Chapter 4

2 to 4 These questions are designed to permit you to develop some of the techniques explained in this chapter on a small scale. Of course, there is no "correct" solution because the techniques depend on the respondents' values and judgments.
5 Selected sources of data are listed in the appendixes at the end of this chapter.

Chapter 5

1 The concept of *stock* refers to *one point* in time and *flow* refers to a *period* of time. Some financial ratios use data from the stock balance sheet and the flow income statement. In order to equate the time periods, the data from two balance sheets are averaged.
2 Explicit recognition must be noted in writing—or verbally—that the ratios are appropriate for a particular phase of the life cycle.
3 Who knows? One number by itself has virtually no meaning. It is like a partial score of a world series ball game. The score is 14 to ? The point is that more data are needed to make a reasonable judgment.
4 Liquidity refers to ability to meet short-term obligations.

Chapter 6

1   Price is independent of the number of units sold.
    Costs are independent of the number of units sold.
    Variable costs change in direct proportion to the number of units sold.
2   50,000
3   High operating leverage and high degrees of financial risk go hand in hand.

Chapter 7

1   (*a*) $1611
    (*b*) $2594
    (*c*) $6728
    (*d*) $17,449
4   (*a*) $857
    (*b*) $743

2   (*a*) $2488
    (*b*) $6192
    (*c*) $38,338
    (*d*) $237,376
5   21.32 percent

Chapter 8

1   Reject.
2   14 percent
3   There are insufficient data to make a valid decision. The IRR could result
    in dollar returns of $1 or $100 million.

Chapter 9

1   See Figure 9-5A.

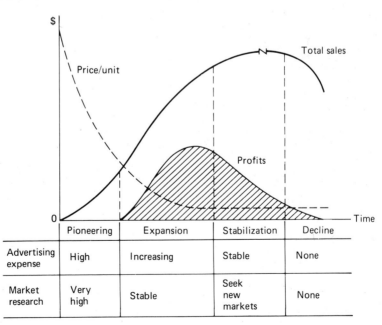

	Pioneering	Expansion	Stabilization	Decline
Advertising expense	High	Increasing	Stable	None
Market research	Very high	Stable	Seek new markets	None

Figure 9-5A

Chapter 9 (*continued*)

2 Customer demand
   Customer growth
   Fuel costs
4 (*a*) 80 percent
   (*b*) 20 percent
5 Cost
   Availability of data
   Time

Chapter 10

1 (*b*) *r*
2 0.14
3 A: $4 per share
   B: $7 per share
   C: $39 per share
5 Be careful in calculating the earnings per share!

Chapter 11

1 Strategy 4, diversification, is the most risky.
   Strategy 1, market penetration, is the least risky.
2 The cost per unit declines 25 percent every time total output doubles. This
   has important strategic implications that are explored in the next question.
4 See Figure 11-7.

Chapter 12

1 Returns refers to expected returns or the most likely return. Risk refers to
   the variability of the expected returns and may be measured by the standard
   deviation of those returns. One may also use other measures of variability.
   However, the standard deviation is commonly used because it can also be
   used in other calculations.
2 Beta is an index of systematic risk. The basic equation for beta was presented
   in Chapter 2.
3 No.
4 Keep in mind their locations on the life cycle.

Chapter 13

1 Stabilization
2 Pioneering

Index

Index